# HOW TO TELL IF YOU'RE AN

# A**HOLE BOSS

## A HUMOROUS, YET HONEST EXPOSÉ ON MISGUIDED MANAGEMENT BEHAVIORS

written by

# TAMICA SEARS

STORYMAKERS, Inc.

Published in 2022 by

STORYMAKERS, INC.
P.O. Box 91338
Houston, Texas 77291-1338
www.storymakersinc.com

ISBN: 978-0-9888079-8-3

Printed in the United States of America

# TABLE OF CONTENTS

# ACKNOWLEDGEMENT

First, a big thank you to Fred Stawitz for saying that I should just go ahead and do this. You made it seem so easy.

Thank you to Misty Batchelder for seeing me through so much. You make the world a better place.

Chris Ogden, my friend and mentor, thank you for putting me on the right path and showing me the difference between a job and a career. And of course, thank you for knowing math.

Toni Botting, without your nepotism and love, I have no idea where I would be.

My Bro in Law Bill who always makes me laugh.

To my first boss, Sheila Mallard, thank you for trusting a high school student with payroll.

Talisa, you are literally my other half. Thank you for being the incognito evil twin so that I can push the envelope in real life and thank you for Max and Mackenzie. They make me want to make the world a better place. Mark's cool too, but he will think that this is a heavy read, so you'll have to summarize it for him.

Tanya, you tried your best. You've always been my cheerleader, thank you.

Thank you to my brother Beasty for being the first and laying the Williams foundation.

Janelle, thank you for being the beautiful perfect person that you are.

My Gina, I will never be able to repay you for the time that you took holding my hand under that tree. You're the absolute best.

Elizabeth, you and Vanessa mean the world to me. I'm so proud of you and happy that you are raising strong women leaders.

Michele, Richard, Gary, Turk you will always have a place in my heart, #traumabonds.

Thank you, Kirsty for proving that internet strangers can be positively life changing. You and Seth are the sister and brother I didn't realize I needed.

Thank you, Lindsay, for being my ride or die. We haven't died yet, so yay!

Darius and TaTiana, I moved across the country because I missed you so much and it was totally worth it.

Tamara and Aiden, I am so lucky to be your aunt.

Cozy, thank you for the shocked look every time I visit, it cracks me up.

Arlandra Lynn, you crazy millennial traveler, thank you for showing me another way of life.

Laurel, thank you for your coaching and for the Institute for Integrative Intelligence. You changed my life and made me a better person.

Aunt Dot, thank you for showing me the world.

My Detroit Aunties, thank you.

Chanel, thank you for making me look good. Literally.

Tom, thank you for all of the Draymond time, the only thing he lets me do is type.

Thank you, Amber, my Strawberry Shortcake, for believing in yourself.

Bob Z, you rock!

Lonni, the world must protect you at all costs. Thank you for being you and for believing in me.

Jason Ross, you're an awesome hype man but an even better EVP, thank you for being a leader that people can look up to.

My SB POC's thank you for keeping me sane. Well sane-ish.

Christine, Abbie, Dan, Glendalynn, Mark, Maureen, Michael, Russ, Zach, Doug, Brian, Roger, and Bobby the Bear, ya'll rock and make LinkedIn fun.

Jamie and Demetra, thank you for all of your help putting this together.

Thank you, Eric the ying to my yang, and best older little brother a girl could ever have!

Alma and James, my mother and father, I miss you both and I couldn't have asked for a better mommy.

And last but most importantly thank you to Troix and Kim, my babies. You push me to do better every day.

# Disclaimer

This book is not meant to be academic in nature, and that should be evident by how often I use the word *asshole*. But I want to put it out there anyway. I'm not an academic like Brené Brown, and in no way should this book be taken as anything as serious as she writes. I don't even have a PhD in *TED Talkery*. However, I have spent years observing and analyzing the leadership behaviors that appear in these pages. The writing is fictionalized and is a mix of different people and situations woven together to tell a story. If you read a story and think it's about you, it actually isn't—but you probably are an *asshole boss*. If not currently, then at some point during your career. In addition, names throughout this work have been fictionalized for obvious reasons.

# Introduction

It is an age-old saying that people don't leave organizations, they leave bosses. In my 20+ years as a Human Resources Professional, I can tell you with absolute certainty this is the case.

Hi, I'm Tamica Sears, and I'm so glad you're here. With my education and experience combined, I'm here to walk you through a self-discovery process that will improve your career as a leader. Sometimes the truth can hurt, but nothing good comes from standing still and burying your head in the sand.

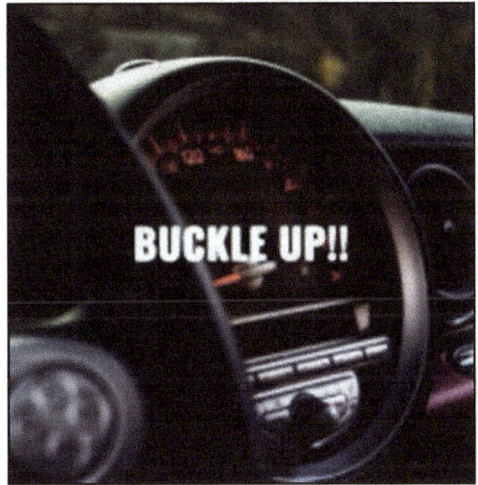

Throughout my career, I've seen amazing leadership, as well as not-so-amazing management. After all, I've been watching leaders do their thing for two decades. In that time, unfortunately, I've worked for some really terrible ones. That's exactly the reason why I'm writing this, so other people aren't put through the kind of horrible experiences I've had. And trust me, I've had some straight-up *asshole bosses*.

I started my career in Human Resources ages ago as an after-school job in high school. Unlike a lot of my peers, we (my twin sister worked there, too) were accepted as part of the team and people went out of their way to show us the ropes. It was fun, I learned a lot, and it launched me into an awesome career. However, it left me totally unprepared for the real world of horrible, awful, *asshole bosses*.

Since my awesome first job, I have worked for multiple companies, large and small in a myriad of industries. I've also had the pleasure of consulting with and coaching executives and emerging leaders all around the country. My hands-on experience, along with my various degrees and certifications helped me put together a framework for my view of what great leadership is and the steps that leaders need to take to get there.

Let me introduce you to the management hierarchy in the Human Resources world. First, we have leaders, then managers, and finally, we have bosses. The truth is people rarely leave their leaders.

But they'll *run* from bad bosses.

## Bad Bosses and Big Losses

Let's break down the hierarchy further. At the top, we have true leaders, people who put their teams before themselves. They give credit where credit is due, they provide timely feedback, and most of all, they genuinely *give a shit*. From my experience, when an employee reports to a leader who honestly and genuinely cares about them, as a person *and* as an employee, it makes all the difference in the world. Trust and loyalty are born. These are the people that we call Kickass Leaders. They are the people that employees flock to and want to work for.

In our next level down, we have managers. Managers are those who sometimes get a little lost. They may try to do the things capable leaders do: they provide feedback, and they want to do what's right for the team. But unlike leaders, they may be out for themselves. They may not trust their team, and they might even pick and choose who they care about on the team. These managers often want to do better, and most of them are doing the work it takes to move up and become great leaders. Once they truly understand that you manage processes and lead people, things start to improve and get better. This group is in the middle, so we are going to call them, of course, Middle Managers.

But at the bottom of the pile, we have bosses. These are the people who take credit for the ideas of others. They openly mistreat people. They don't trust their teams, and their teams don't trust them. These bosses may not even realize how bad things are because they lack the necessary self-awareness to understand how their behavior impacts others. They only care about themselves and most times, they truly do not give a single *shit* about their team. Those are the bad bosses. For the purposes of this book and to not confuse anyone who might still be living in the 90's and think that *bad* means *good*, we're going to spruce up the title and call bad bosses by their proper name: *Asshole Bosses*.

For our three management levels, consider the following characteristics:

- **Kickass Leaders** know their behavior directly impacts their employees, and they don't want to jeopardize those relationships. They do what they can to maintain trusting and transparent relationships with their team.

- **Middle Managers** sometimes lose their way, but they understand how important it is to treat people well. Sometimes, they just don't know how to achieve that.

xvii

- **Asshole Bosses** think they know what they're doing, but they don't. And remember, employees leave bad bosses. They will literally quit with no notice and moonwalk out, holding up both middle fingers.

What's the bottom line? Good leaders typically have happy employees. Bad bosses don't.

And let's face it; happy employees just don't look for other jobs.

Listen, I get it. It's not easy being in charge. "With great power comes great responsibility," and when you're leading people, you carry nearly unending responsibilities.

That means you must bear the "brunt of badness" on your shoulders, so it doesn't trickle down. It's part of your job to protect your employees. You also must translate messages from above and own them. Not to mention that you're expected to demonstrate the vision and mission of your organization and at least give the appearance you know what it takes to get there.

But when any of these pieces of your job aren't carried out consistently, employees lose faith, motivation, and productivity. And those buy-ins are nearly impossible to get back once they're gone. Trust is hard to win but very, very easy to lose.

Most of this seems like common sense, I know. However, more often than you'd believe, I stumble across a manager who just doesn't get it.

- A manager who thinks fear or intimidation is the best way to get things done.
- A manager who thinks it's their way or the highway.
- A manager who thinks getting to know their employees is the highest level of unprofessionalism.

Let me tell you: those people are not leaders. They are not managers. They are bosses.

And most of them are *asshole bosses*.

As you can probably guess, *asshole bosses* are bad for business. They typically have unproductive teams filled with miserable people and high turnover. And as I've pointed out, most *asshole bosses* don't even realize they are *asshole bosses*.

That's where I come in. I have put together a foolproof way to tell if you are, in fact, an *asshole boss*.

As we move forward, keep in mind that I don't have a PhD in *Manager Tomfoolery*. Nor have I spent ten years in academia researching leadership behavior. But what I can share is my in-the-trenches experience. I've been in Human Resources for over 20 years in multiple organizations and across a myriad of industries.

As you read through this book, you might start to recognize yourself in some of the sections. You may determine you *are* an *asshole boss*. It's not an easy realization. But knowledge is power, my friend.

That's why I'm here, to help you move away from being an *asshole boss* and become a leader who employees will respect and follow. With proper management and leadership, employees will be inspired to give you their best.

If you are really willing to put in the time and effort, I can even help you become a leader. A strong leader. It's a challenging and oftentimes bumpy road but as with all things worth having, determination and practice will pay off in abundance.

So, let's get started. First things first. I've identified some clues you can reflect on in your career as a manager.

If you can see yourself reflected in these clues, you may be an *asshole boss*.

# YOU ENTER A ROOM, AND PEOPLE STOP TALKING

Whenever you arrive at the office, do you get the cold shoulder? Does the atmosphere go from warm and friendly to awkward and quiet? Does everyone turn off their camera on Zoom when you join the call?

It's a regular Monday morning, and people are loading up with caffeine and donuts in the breakroom, preparing for the week ahead. They're chatting, laughing, and catching each other up on their news from the weekend. You feel energized by their happy mood and enter the room with a smile on your face.

But instead of the happy greetings you expected, people stop talking.

All of a sudden, they seem incredibly fascinated by the contents of their coffee cups.

Others look at the floor and mutter a muted *"good morning"* (with all of the enthusiasm of a turnip). Shockingly enough, a few people even hastily leave the room.

What is going on? I mean, you've *tried* engaging them in conversation before. You always offer a hearty *"Good morning, everyone!"*

The employees not only don't reciprocate, but you're usually met with silence. You're puzzled and annoyed by their reaction (or lack of it).

*What is their problem, anyway?*

If this has happened to you as a manager, it's frustrating and confusing.

Or consider this scenario. It's Friday, late in the afternoon, after a super long week. Your team has busted their butts and pulled off something extraordinary. You're looking forward to going home to relax and relish in the successes of the week.

But on your way out, a small group from your team hops on the elevator with you. They start talking about how great their celebratory lunch was. Obviously, they're talking about the team achievements this week.

You're irked. You think to yourself, *"What lunch?!"*

No one invited you to any lunch. Evidently, your team has celebrated without you. *Without its leader!*

First of all, I want to assure you that you aren't alone.

Each manager who experiences difficulties like this has arrived there confused and probably without meaning to. Let me explain what I mean.

Some managers *really care* about not being liked. About being excluded. They view being excluded as a big problem. But other managers don't care. And therein lies a bigger problem.

# Manager, Meet Reality

To demonstrate this, I'll share a real-life example I encountered. I once worked with a manager named Rebecca, who believed managers weren't allowed to have personal conversations with the people who worked for them.

On top of that, Rebecca referred to her team as "her staff," which was a dead giveaway—this leader had no idea how to deal with people. This was, after all, the 21st century. We are supposed to be in a time of innovation and equality. We are well past the days of *Downton Abbey* with lowly servants living downstairs having nothing better to do but serve the English ruling class living upstairs. Unfortunately, many managers like Rebecca view and treat their team as minions to get the job done.

Time for a reality check.

Rebecca, *the Asshole Boss*, wanted her team to tell her every little detail about anything related to work, but she never asked her employees a single personal question. One of her employees even said they were surprised Rebecca even knew their names and didn't just use their employee numbers.

Is that *really* the way anyone wants to be viewed?

Like with all managers that I work with, Rebecca and I sat down quite often and I got to know her pretty well. Over time, during these meetings she revealed quite a bit. Rebecca didn't understand why she wasn't well-liked. She didn't realize at all how others perceived her. She was living smack dab in the middle of the town of "I Don't Know What I Don't Know." It sucks there.

Thankfully, I understood how her employees were feeling.

A manager can't hide this kind of attitude from their team. Employees *know* when the manager supposedly "leading them" has zero interest in learning who they are as people. Consequently, employees don't see the point of talking to their manager about anything.

An *asshole boss* like Rebecca simply wouldn't care.

# Nobody's Fool

Employees aren't dummies. They know the same manager doesn't care about their career development, either. As a result, whether Rebecca's door was open or closed, employees didn't care. Either Rebecca's opinion didn't matter, or the employees weren't interested in talking to her about anything. They simply kept their heads down and did their job, most times, pretty poorly, unfortunately. They also stopped talking whenever Rebecca showed up.

I'm here to tell you that it's definitely a red flag if your team doesn't talk to you openly. If you don't care that they don't talk to you openly, it's an even bigger red flag.

At this point, it doesn't matter how you got into this predicament. You need to fix it ASAP!

And let me warn you, it most likely won't be an easy, overnight solution.

After all, you haven't gotten to this place overnight. You've probably lost the trust and possibly the respect of your staff over time. After many encounters that always ended up the same, they may no longer view you as credible and supportive, both understandable reasons for them to stop talking when you enter the room.

And it's difficult to tell you this, but it doesn't even matter if you *think* you've done everything right up until now. In your mind, your employees are just difficult people who expect coddling.

But at this point, you simply can't afford to play the blame game. You need to start asking yourself some tough questions and giving yourself some honest answers.

If your employees tend to clam up when you're around, let's look at some potential reasons.

## Reasons Employees Avoid You

No matter who they are, what their role is, people who work 40+ hours a week *want* to like their job, co-workers, and leaders. They *want* to connect with others in the workplace, have a successful career and *feel valued* for their contributions.

So, when your employees don't appear open to you or your ideas, you might wonder if you're in the *Twilight Zone*.

In this section, we'll talk about some of the reasons employees might avoid talking to you. If you see yourself in any of these, hang on for the tips later in this chapter. I've got you.

### 1. Does your office maintain a cold, professional culture?

When caring only appears to happen *outside* of work, distrust and discomfort are the results. As a manager, you want to maintain a professional culture, but there can still be warmth toward your employees who are, in fact, real people with unique talents and gifts.

After all, without employees, you don't have a job.

A cold and negative workplace culture can include a wide variety of elements, but in this instance, let's focus on a culture of extreme "professionalism." You may think this is the right way to go but creating a sterile, bland, and boring place of work isn't what employees need. This type of atmosphere gives your employees no reason to try. Really, why should they strive for quality when they are seen as just a cog in a wheel?

Simply put, an uber-professional, no-nonsense environment creates an unhealthy culture. And employees in an unhealthy workplace culture have less motivation and are more likely to leave. It'll also be much harder for the company to attract and keep new talent. These environments often leave employees feeling faceless, and nameless, with them doing all of the work while others take the credit, along with any bonuses or extra compensation that comes with a job well done.

But in an open workplace culture, employees believe in the company vision and embrace their role in reaching that goal. They feel respected and trusted. They build connections with their team members.

In a healthy work environment, employees see managers eliminate negative behaviors, people who behave badly or perform poorly are coached and if things don't get better, they are terminated. In a healthy work environment, good employees are celebrated for doing well. They feel

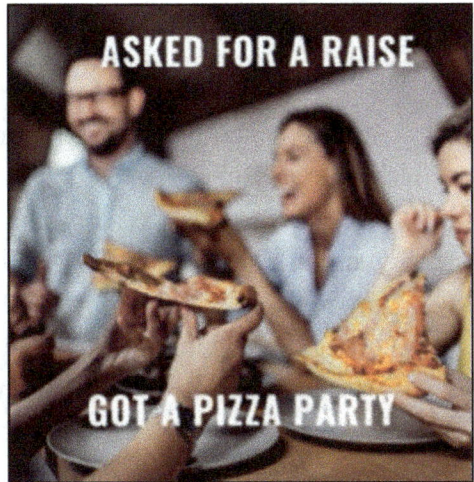

safe when a manager enters the room. And much of this comes from seeing leaders who actually *walk the walk.*

You'll need to ask yourself if your leadership style contributes to a negative atmosphere:

- *Is profit prioritized over people?*
- *Is the bottom line more important than ethical behavior?*
- *Is micromanagement the norm?*

Remember what you promote is what influences your employees and their behavior. Promote an open culture, and you're more likely to create trusting employees.

And trusting employees are more likely to smile and greet you warmly when you enter the room.

## 2. Are you too talkative?

Instead of not ever having conversations on a personal level, are you the only one getting personal? In other words, if you don't give your employees a chance to talk and be heard—they're likely to shut down after an unsuccessful attempt or two. This could be why they stop talking and don't want to give you the time of day.

It may have happened without you realizing it. Perhaps a worker comes to you with one quick question. But you respond, "Sure, hang on. Ah, there we go. Sorry. I just need to get this email finished. You wouldn't believe the day I've had. My kid failed college chemistry, my roof was damaged by hail last night, and my hubby wants to sell our house just to buy one three times more expensive. Who has time or energy for that? Or the money to pay for it, for that matter. And the puppy, oh my God! He can destroy a pair of stilettos in no time flat. It's all an absolute nightmare. And to top it off, I'm not sleeping at night."

Your employee smiles politely but shifts uncomfortably in their chair. Do you realize what just happened?

What began as a simple question on the employee's part has become a counseling session for *you*. Suddenly, they're getting a recap of your life, but they're too polite to point out that you talk too much. While this kind of sharing can be enjoyable during after-work get-togethers, it's exhausting for your employees when they're in "the zone" of doing the work they should be doing to get you and your team past the finish line.

Or maybe you talk about employees to other employees. A manager who talks behind one employee's back will do the same to all employees. Let me tell you, this is more than a sticky situation. It's *mortal sin #1* for a manager.

If you disregard your employee's confidence, I feel obligated to inform you this is inappropriate, unacceptable, and unethical. And you're absolutely an *asshole boss*.

For example, if an employee requests vacation time because her teenage son is in legal trouble, this is *not* up for group discussion at the next staff meeting. Mum's the word. You must be a vault that refuses to reveal personal details your employees shared with you in confidence.

I've even heard of managers who asked employees to spy on their colleagues and report back. Do I even need to explain why this is a disaster waiting to happen? Well, I guess I do because it *does* happen.

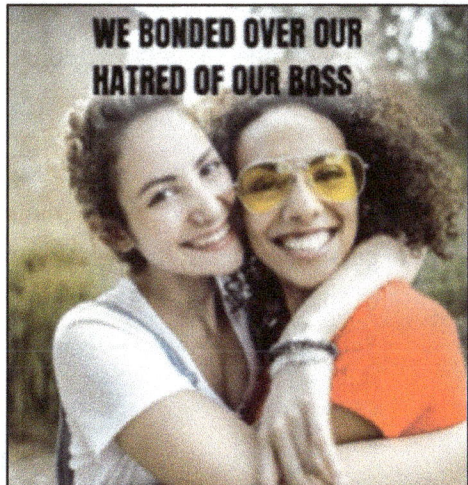

Your job as a leader is to keep the pulse on your team. That isn't something you can delegate. And if you do, there will be problems. How can you ever expect someone to trust you after you've asked them to spy on a co-worker? Even worse, what if they find out you've asked someone to spy on *them*?

I'll say it hundreds—or even thousands—of times. If your team doesn't trust you, they will not be a high-performing team. Ever. They will never function at the top of their capacity as they'll spend time and energy on trivial office gossip and politics if you pit them against each other.

If you feel like doing this, guess what? Yep, you're an *asshole boss*.

Managers, avoid oversharing, resist overtalking, and refuse to betray an employee's confidence. These tips alone will better prepare you to win over the trust of your employees, prompting them to open up when you waltz into the room.

### 3. As a manager, do you show any curiosity about your employees and their lives?

People want to be seen. Yes, their work accomplishments should consistently be acknowledged and celebrated, but what about their personal lives?

A marriage, birth, adoption, divorce, surgery, serious diagnosis, or death of a loved one signals significant shifts in an employee's personal life. Acknowledging an employee's circumstances outside of their career shows personal concern. It demonstrates that they're valued beyond their contribution to the team. We'll talk more about this in Chapter 2.

It's entirely possible to maintain a level of professionalism and productivity while showing empathy and compassion.

And it's been proven that when employees have these life events, they are at a higher risk of looking for a new job. This is because of the same type of thought processes that are causing so many people to resign during "The Great Resignation." People start to evaluate their lives during birthdays and anniversaries. Big life events make people take stock of their surroundings. And if their surroundings include a horrible work environment, they start looking to make a change. Want to prevent that? Consider the following tips:

- **You have to be vulnerable** first, which increases the likelihood of an employee coming to you during a personal upheaval. On the flip side, if you are in the midst of a difficult situation, like a death in the family or another crisis, you need to be vulnerable and *let your team know* you're going through a rough time.

- **Recognize the warning signs of an employee who is struggling.** If you've built a good team relationship, it will be easier to detect problems early on. If you don't know the signs, ask for help so you can acquire that skill immediately. If your HR team can't help you with this, if they can't, google SAMHSA.

- **Don't pry or act as the office therapist.** You can care without pushing and asking uncomfortable questions. Since you hold more power, employees may tell you more than they're comfortable with, so be sure to set boundaries.

- **Listen first.** *Really* listen. Use eye contact. Use open body language. Then, ask questions like *"How can we support you?"* or *"What can we do, if anything, to help you?"*

- **Consider their workload and what adjustments can be made.** Be sure to reward those who step up to help out. Remember, when you are divvying up the work, don't divulge any confidential information about an employee. You also shouldn't share why they're getting the extra work without the explicit permission of the person they are covering for ... preferably in *writing*.

11

As for the happy events in an employee's life, you want to *show up!* Celebrate work anniversaries, birthdays, personal life achievements, family events and milestones, and National Employee Appreciation Day (the first Friday in March). These are just no-brainers when it comes to demonstrating an employee's value. The heart of your leadership should be authentically leading your employees. If you know them, you know what they actually want.

Simply caring about an employee's life outside of work goes so far in building trust. People want to talk to managers who actively care about their lives!

As a side note, thank you notes aren't dead. A handwritten note shows genuine effort and appreciation in our digital world and would build bridges with your employees.

## 4. Is the office environment intimidating?

If you're eyeing your employees each time they take a personal call or stop at a co-worker's desk to chat, you're sending the message that you disapprove of them and their behavior. Yes, work should be at the forefront, but everyone needs some time to connect. Does anything about your office environment say, *let's have a real conversation?*

## 5. Is the focus on busyness over relationships?

Okay, results are vital. In any business environment, there are goals. Managers are usually responsible for making sure the goals are met. Consider this: someone may look busy, but they're actually shopping online during work hours; while someone having a personal conversation could be building a very valuable working relationship with a peer. Looks can be deceiving and if you are basing your opinions about someone's "busyness" based on what you think you see; you could be way off base. Getting things done is very important, but relationships are just as beneficial, so again, I say: you should lead by example. It's more than saying "*Good morning!*" as you fill your coffee cup. Have an actual conversation. Would you rather your team just look busy, or do their actual work cheerfully?

### 6. Are you coming across as an insecure manager?

Managers who are uncomfortable make their employees uncomfortable too. Unfortunately, this behavior can be perceived as insecurity on your part. If you don't understand your expectations as a manager or lack the training to be a strong leader, go to your manager and ask for help. Remember, it's a sign of strength to ask for help, not a weakness. Employees need a leader they can confidently follow and trust.

We talked a bit about work culture in the list above, but let's investigate more closely to create a culture that will boost your trustworthiness and reliability as a manager. Achieving these milestones can lead your employees to chat with you about their lives at work and outside of work.

# Creating a Fair and Inviting Work Culture

First, make sure you **promote inclusivity and diversity**. It's simply vital that individuals from all backgrounds are accepted and celebrated. Inclusive language should be modeled, and diversity initiatives should be promoted. In fact, if your company isn't diverse, diversity should become a huge focus in your company's recruitment strategies. As a leader, you can set the example by embracing everyone and fostering an environment where everyone feels like they belong. If you haven't already done that, there's one clue as to why your company isn't as diverse as it could be. Learn to celebrate differences rather than seeing these as negative things.

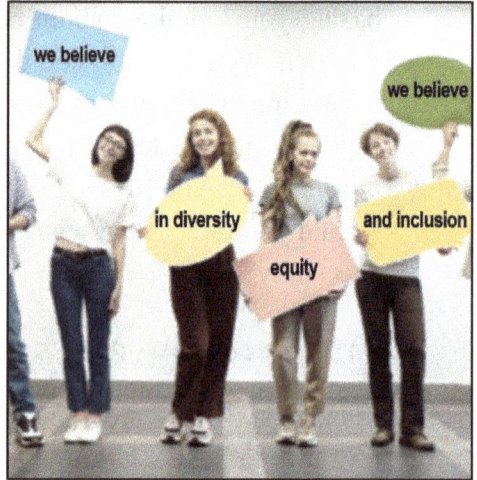

Next, **allow humor**. We all know how stressful work can be. Most of us would agree that humor brings a positive outlook and fresh perspective. Dale Carnegie, an American writer and lecturer once said, "People rarely succeed unless they're having fun in what they're doing." With this in mind, find the bright side, and make sure your employees know you're there. The reward is they'll trust you and work even harder for you. A note of caution, though: allowing humor is not the same as permitting bad behavior like unnecessary or unkind mocking about other employees. Never allow mean or petty conduct in the name of being funny.

As you joke around, remember that there is a fine line. Don't be corny, and don't try to make getting a laugh mandatory. If someone is belly-laughing at your dad jokes, you may not be as funny as you think you are. If you call a lion a fibbing cat, don't expect people to double over with laughter.

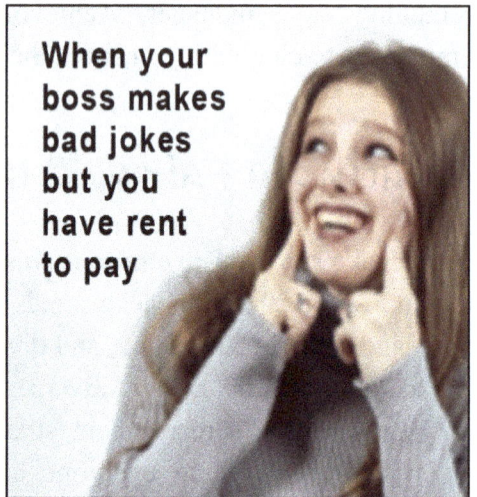

Third, **place a priority on respect**. From the janitor to the CEO and all the interns in between, treat everyone with respect. After all, there's room at the table for everyone. Respect can be communicated in two ways: verbally and nonverbally. Accordingly, beyond the words you choose, be aware of your body language and what it's communicating. By making them respect the rule, you're allowing your employees to share their ideas and thoughts in a safe space.

> **PRO TIP**
>
> When it comes to nonverbal communications, consider the following: avoid crossing your arms, pay attention to facial expressions, and use eye contact.

Fourth, ensure you have a **zero-tolerance policy for bad behavior** in place. Employees should be protected in your workplace. As such, you need to make sure that you have a clearly written policy that forbids any type of harassment in the workplace. Then, invite your employees to provide input on ways to improve; by doing so, you're removing barriers that prevent employees from sharing their thoughts and concerns. As you can imagine, employees also need to feel safe in expressing issues, and confident that they'll be provided the necessary resources and support. Along with your HR team, (preferably with their direction) you should investigate every allegation of misconduct.

You'll also want to offer harassment prevention and proper reporting training to all employees. As a side note, requiring sexual harassment training is a wise move, even if your state doesn't insist on periodic training. Again, get with your HR team about this and make sure it's getting done. Because by providing a zero-tolerance environment, you're building your credibility and trustworthiness.

Fifth, **welcome, accept, and use feedback from your employees**. Some managers bristle at the idea of employee feedback, but good managers think of feedback as a way to make the company, and sometimes themselves, better. Remember, feedback isn't necessarily about what you're doing wrong. Instead, it allows employees to share their pain points (and we all need to share those every once in a while). And chances are, employees aren't alone in their struggles. By openly welcoming feedback, you gain valuable insight. Then, you can make necessary adjustments and ensure success for the entire team. Ask them what is going well and what isn't. Doing a *Start, Stop, Continue* exercise frequently can be useful (more on that later).

Finally, **be flexible**. Allow your employees to be human. If someone is struggling, work with them. Compromise. Help them be productive at work. For example, maybe 9 to 5 isn't working for one of your employees, but they're working diligently no matter what hours they work. When possible, be open to a different schedule. In a case like this, everyone wins. Otherwise, you will seem unapproachable or unaccommodating when issues come up. And remember, allowing flexible schedules helps with employee retention overall.

# Bringing It All Together

We've covered a lot in this section. We've considered why employees might not feel safe talking to you, and we've given some tips to make them feel safe and secure in opening up to you. Let's review those valuable clues:

1. *Do you have a cold and intimidating office environment?*
2. *Are you talking too much when you should be listening?*
3. *Are you sharing care and concern for your employees outside of work?*

4. *Are you sending signals that intimidate employees?*
5. *Do you focus on busyness over relationships?*
6. *Do you convey insecurity rather than confidence?*

We then gave you some suggestions:

- promote diversity and inclusion
- allow humor
- prioritize respect
- enforce a zero-tolerance policy for bad behavior
- welcome feedback from employees
- be flexible when it comes to compromising with employees

If you recognize yourself in any of the problems mentioned, you might be wondering where to start. Have no fear! The following section helps you reflect on your leadership style and offers solutions for improvement, so you have a team that trusts you and talks to you.

# Self-Reflection & Solutions

It's time to look at yourself as a leader, so consider the following questions. But first, take a step back and give yourself a moment for a deep breath or two.

Now, look at your intentions truthfully:

- *How do you reward your employees for a job well done?*
- *What do you do to celebrate team and individual successes?*
- *When was the last time you took the team out for lunch or paid for the first round at happy hour?*
- *Do you praise your team loudly and often?*
- *Are you walking into conversations with your employees assuming positive intent?*

17

Once you've considered these, let me share a valuable insight: leadership is no longer about command and control. *It's about treating people like people.*

Here's a suggestion to get your leadership reputation moving in the right direction.

> **TIP 1**
>
> Hold frequent one-on-one meetings with your employees.

A good rule of thumb to keep in mind for an employee one-on-one includes the following:

- 10 minutes for them
- 10 minutes for you
- 10 minutes to pour into their career/personal development

Consider these tips to best prepare for employee one-on-one meetings that are productive and beneficial for each party:

1. Having consistent **talking points** prepared can help the meetings flow more easily.

2. Send a calendar invite, so you both get reminders the meeting is coming up. Make it a positive experience and mention you're looking forward to your conversations with them.

3. **Do your prep work.** Think about what you've talked about with this employee previously. List some qualities and skills you admire about this employee and be prepared to share them at your first meeting. Showing appreciation is like giving oxygen to employees.

Going forward, it's essential to let them know where they stand. No one should leave that meeting without a clear understanding of how they are doing on the job.

Here are some suggestions for talking points to guide you during an employee one-on-one:

- *Tell me what your best day at work looks like. What are you doing? And not doing?*
- *Let's imagine your best day at work is a 10 and an average day is a 5. In comparison, how would your typical day be rated?*
- *For your typical day, you choose a _____. Tell me more about why you chose that number.*
- *To get that number closer to 10, what would you need? Let's try to come up with three different ideas or tasks to try.*
- *Of the three ideas you provided, which one would you prefer to start with over the next two or three weeks?*
- *What obstacles can I clear for you?*
- *How can I help you?*

**PRO TIP**

If you can't follow through with an employee's request for help or find someone who can, make sure to get back to your employee and let them know.

- *In your opinion, what should I be asking you?*
- *Is there something you want me to ask about that I haven't thought of?*
- *What are you working on for your professional development?*
- *What are you working on for your personal development?*
- *What are some of the upcoming projects that seem interesting to you?*
- *What are your priorities?*

- *What are your career goals, and what can I do to help you with them?*
- *How are you?*

    Yes, you can and should use these three simple words with your employees.

These meetings should help your employees know what they should be working on, how well they are doing, and what you can contribute to help them be successful. At the same time, this doesn't have to be *just* a work-focused meeting. Spend this time getting to know your employee better. Make it a priority. And don't double book or move the meeting around each week. Always be on time. That meeting is an extension of your employee, so treat it right.

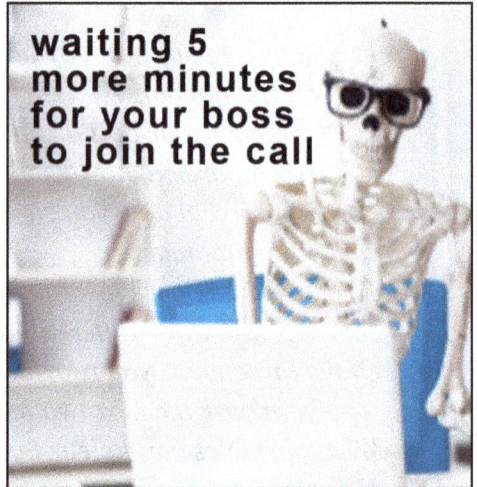

waiting 5 more minutes for your boss to join the call

At the end of your one-on-one, it's necessary to ask for feedback. Successful leaders strive to make progress, so be sure to ask how the next one-on-one meeting could improve. Doing so also shows you value their opinions, a vital factor in trust.

Most employees crave social interaction. Even those introverts who are shy in large groups have their own interests and want to belong. Provide chances for employees to get to know each other—and you—outside of work responsibilities.

Consider offering activities like a running club, team competition, or a Friday afternoon happy hour hosted by the company. Beyond your own ideas, though, ask employees what they'd like, because remember, this isn't about you. Be prepared to hear all kinds of ideas, from online gaming competitions or organized book clubs to volunteer opportunities or a good old-fashioned round of dodgeball. Which, by the way, is probably not a regular activity at elementary schools anymore and perhaps for a good reason.

> **2** **PART**
>
> Do something fun.

I hear you whining, but *we're remote nowwwww!* So what? It just means you have to get creative. For example, did you know there are online escape rooms now? In fact, there are tons of remote team-building ideas. Like with everything else, Google is your friend. Put in the work and figure out what works for you and your team.

Outside of work hours, you might have a group who wants to run a marathon together—competition is actually good for a team! Perhaps a few employees want to improve their cooking skills or take an art class. Maybe you even have a few singers in the group who'd love a good karaoke night. You could have sports fans who want to tailgate the next game together.

Keep in mind that as varied as a team of employees can be, there are endless options for fun. Developing a group that likes each other—and you— increases productivity and benefits the company all around. And it gives them something to talk to you about in the break room.

Allowing downtime or bonding time for employees can often be difficult for managers, but force yourself to think of team building as *real work* instead of wasted work time. Remember, the goal is to get your employees to open up and trust you, and bringing your people together as a team moves you in that direction. Building team morale at the same time is just the icing on the cake.

One last note—make sure the company pays for all team-building activities. No employee out there wants to be forced to participate and then pony up their own money to do it. When possible and appropriate, you should also invite significant others and kids.

Team building is an investment in your team as the unique people they are. When they feel valued and like you've put time, energy and other resources into them, they're more apt to talk to you in the break room, and more likely to be happy at work and do their job well.

| M A P T I P | Ask your leader how you're doing. |
|---|---|

For now, a good start is to have a conversation with your leader, who hopefully isn't an *asshole boss*, about how you're performing. It may sound daunting, but you can't change what you don't know about, and in most situations, you don't know how your leader perceives you unless you ask. This is the first step in a more comprehensive process, a 360 Leadership Assessment.

A 360 Leadership Assessment is often the fastest and easiest way to understand what's going well and what's not going so well on your team. This assessment evaluates you as a leader. A good one will tell you a lot about your productivity and performance by soliciting feedback from your leader, direct reports, and peers.

Generally speaking, your leadership style may have started with good intentions, but what matters is the actual impact on others. Doing this assessment helps you understand if your style is working for you or against you. We'll go more into detail on 360 Leadership Assessments in Chapter 8. For now, a good start is to have that open conversation and ask questions like:

- *How am I doing?*
- *What are your thoughts on my leadership style?*
- *What is one thing that you can recommend that I work on to become a better leader?*

Michael Scott of *The Office* once said, "Would I rather be feared or loved? Easy. Both. I want people to be afraid of how much they love me."

Okay, you don't have to take it that far, but do strive to be approachable and available to your team. By using these tips, you're well on your way to having team members who value your feedback, praise, and effort. Just like in any relationship, these factors will lead to better communication and trust.

do you love me so much it scares you

Hopefully, your days of being shunned in the break room will soon be a thing of the past. Implement the recommendations in this chapter, and rock on with your bad self.

# YOU DON'T KNOW MUCH ABOUT YOUR EMPLOYEES' LIVES

Who has kids? Who likes skiing? Who's golfing this weekend? As a manager, do you know the answers to these types of questions?

If you've ever experienced a significant life event that goes wholly unnoticed or unacknowledged by your manager, you know what a terrible feeling it is.

Let me provide an example from my own life, one so painful and raw that I'll never forget it. When I was in my early twenties, my mother passed away unexpectedly. It was a total shock, and I was still quite young and had a toddler at the time. I desperately needed my mother and felt like my entire world was collapsing.

Much from that time is a blur, but I remember calling my manager and letting her know what happened. I informed her that I wouldn't be at work for a while. There isn't much I remember during those early days of intense grief, but what I do remember is once I got back to work, my peers were very kind, offered me their condolences, and provided a listening ear.

From my boss, though, I got *nothing*, and that really hurt.

Nearly two decades later, it still stings.

As bad as that was, one of my sisters fared even worse when she returned to her job.

Our mother's death was such a traumatic experience. As a result, my sister wasn't sleeping well, and she became forgetful. Upon returning to the office, her boss called her in to talk. My sister was hoping her boss would offer more time off or provide information for where she could turn for help.

But it was neither of those things. In fact, it was to sign a verbal warning for my sister's performance slipping from outstanding to mediocre.

*What an asshole! Who does that?*

Give that a minute to let it sink in. Honestly. *Who does that?* An *asshole boss*, that's who.

Here's another example of a manager not caring about their employees' lives. For this scenario, imagine you're the manager.

# A Clueless Chief

You're at a staff meeting. Jim enters the conference room and takes a seat. Everyone there starts congratulating him, but you have no clue what Jim has done to receive such accolades. You begin to wonder if he finished that project you assigned him. Did he somehow go over your head and present it?!

Nonchalantly, you continue to listen. You soon find out Jim's wife gave birth to twins a few weeks ago, and this is his first day back in the office.

Honestly, you had no clue Jim was even out of the office, much less a new father to twins. How did that slip by you? Now you're worried you look like you're either clueless or uncaring for not offering congratulations.

If this is you, my friend, I have sad news. You are both: clueless and uncaring. And probably an *asshole boss*.

You certainly aren't expected to know *everything* about *every* employee in your company, but if you have an employee out on leave, you should take the time to find out why.

Employees often complain that their managers don't listen to them, spend time with them, include them in important meetings, do performance reviews consistently, or have empathy for an employee's work-life balance. *Ouch!*

In addition, managers often appear to totally disregard when employees face challenging times, caring only about the work output. But here's the cold, hard truth. If you don't care about your employees as people, they won't care about you. And when that happens, the whole organization suffers.

# Your Leadership as a Catalyst for Change

You, my friend, must be the catalyst for change.

Change must happen through intentional actions, not just words. Show don't tell. Caring about your team members leads to trust, which creates loyalty. The days of expecting employees to leave their personal lives at the door when they arrive at work are long gone.

So, when it comes to life-changing events like weddings, births, deaths, or serious illnesses, you should make it a point to be in the loop. More than that, you should care about employees and their circumstances.

Managers, the importance of this support, particularly during difficult times, cannot be overstated. One of the biggest challenges you might face as a leader is managing employees who are going through personal crises. Even though there's a line between an employee's personal and professional life, handling these situations properly will be a real test of your leadership skills. Your leadership during these times will influence how your employees feel when you enter their space.

I know what you might be thinking, and we're actually going to cover that in a bit. It's possible to show concern and care *without crossing any lines*. In fact, you should be more concerned about coming across as a distant authoritarian, which increases suspicion, poor performance, dissatisfaction, and turnover.

If you wonder why you don't care about your employee's lives, look internally first:

- *Do you care about these types of events in your own life?*
- *If you don't care, why not?*
- *Have you always felt that way?*

- *What changed?*

If you actually do care, do people know you that?

- *Do you ask people questions about themselves?*
- *Do you share information about yourself?*

No matter how you answer these questions, employees will eventually find another boss who supports them if you don't.

*If you're not that into them, don't expect that they'll be into you.*

If your employees feel undervalued or unimportant, how could they trust you'd put in a good word for them when it's time for an evaluation, promotion, or salary increase?

Two words: *they can't!*

So as inconvenient and time-consuming as job searches are today, an unhappy employee will still choose job-seeking over putting up with a boss who just doesn't care. Some might even choose to tighten the purse strings and drive for Uber rather than putting up with a boss who doesn't care. It's your responsibility to show team members that you value them as an employee and as a person.

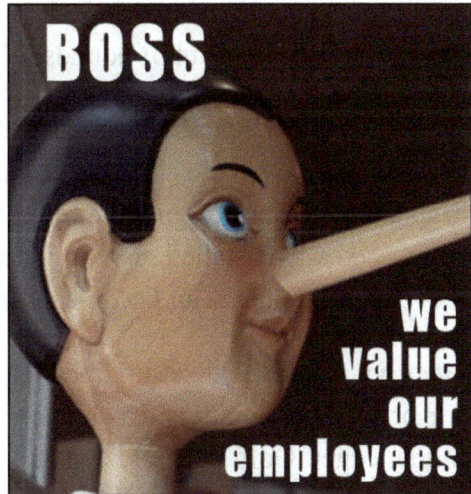

29

Part of that is making sure employees are fairly and equitably compensated. Getting a tiny raise and knowing your manager didn't fight for you is soul-crushing. It would drive anyone away.

Again, *show*—not tell.

With this in mind, let's discuss appropriate boundaries between managers and employees while still showing care and concern for your team members.

# Boundary Basics

What's a boundary, anyway? In technical terms, it's something indicating bounds or limits. In sports, for instance, boundaries mark the exercise mat for gymnasts and their floor performances. This mat is 39 feet x 39 feet, and gymnasts must stay within those boundaries while flipping, tumbling, and dancing. If they step out of bounds, it's a deduction from their score.

For homeowners, boundaries mark the lines of a property. Maybe boundary disputes arise over the years as a bush expands over the fence line or a sizable tree begins dropping large limbs in the neighbor's yard. Or perhaps a new shed was installed next door that infringes on another property. The boundary battle here can become expensive.

Other boundaries that set up lines are everywhere: traffic lights tell you to stop or go. The shoulder on a highway tells you that you're driving too close to the edge. Golf courses, tennis courts, and football fields all have boundaries for the game. No matter what type of boundary we're talking about, they're necessary to recognize.

More than that, they can sometimes become legal issues and lead to devastating consequences when violated. Likewise, in a professional environment, some boundaries shouldn't be crossed. With that in mind, while I want you to care about your employees, I don't want you to *care about your employees*. Know what I mean?

A lack of boundaries can lead to a host of very-bad, no-good consequences:

- misunderstandings
- miscommunication
- resentment
- declining productivity
- decreasing performance
- increasing conflict
- harassment
- job loss

As you can see, certain behaviors aren't acceptable. And just so there's no room for misinterpretation, I want to be very clear in the next section about the no-nos associated with leader-employee relationships. Keep in mind this section assists in knowing your employees and their lives in a way that works for both of you and keeps everyone out of trouble.

# DON'Ts for Leaders

Unfortunately, the lack of boundaries opens the door to a lack of respect. And it invites a lot more than that in a work environment, so take a look at my recommendations for avoiding problems with your team, which can come from not having any boundaries in place:

## 1. Be mindful when you socialize outside of work hours.

Try not to go out with an employee to a bar on a Saturday night unless the entire team is there. Instead, keep that kind of socialization to lunches, happy hours, and holiday parties. And when you're socializing at a team event, talk to everyone, so all employees feel included. And always buy the first round!

2. **Don't drink excessive alcohol at company events like business trips, conferences, and office parties.**

We've all heard the stories of the person who got wildly drunk at the Christmas party and decided to skinny dip in the boss's pool. Don't be that person. And if your company does drug testing, stay away from even legalized drugs! Doing those types of activities with your team can

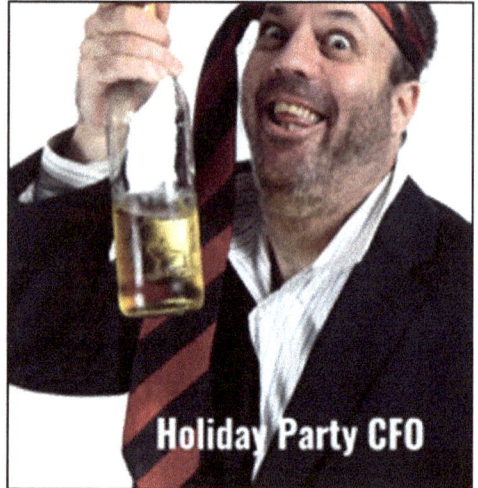

Holiday Party CFO

jeopardize your job and theirs. It's just not worth the risk.

3. **Don't be afraid to share personal information.**

You can share some information with your team members, but remember your audience. Your team doesn't need to hear about the intimate details of your love life or lack thereof. Don't hand your phone over and ask the people who work for you to swipe right. Still, letting people know you on a personal level is crucial to your success. Don't force anyone to reciprocate, meaning if someone doesn't want to share their personal information or details, that's okay. If you keep doing the right things, they may come around. And if not, that's okay, too. Don't treat that person any different than the rest of your team. Some people are just more discreet than others.

Remember how we talked about diversity and inclusion? This fits into that category. I talked a lot about what not to say, but there are more things that you can talk about than there are that are off limits. You can talk about your family, most hobbies, most pets. Read the room and if you have overshared or said something that struck a nerve, acknowledge, apologize, and move on.

## 4. Don't avoid team meetings.

Even if you trust your team and have built a relationship, they still need your leadership. Recurring meetings allow for frequent check-ins. Touching base centers attention back on organizational goals. One of the complaints I repeatedly hear as an HR professional is that when leaders reschedule meetings, don't have them, or don't take them seriously, it speaks volumes to the team and not in a good way. Instead, it's damaging because it comes off like the leader doesn't care about their team. It also leads to massive communication issues.

## 5. Don't let your temper flare.

If there's an issue with an employee, be sure to speak to them privately and calmly. Provide clear feedback on what they did wrong and give helpful guidance for moving forward. I once worked for a company where managers were said to bang on tables and yell at people. Whenever I heard that, I thought of a comedian I once saw. She said that one day, she wanted to punch her boss during their one-on-one meeting. She said people wouldn't believe anyone would do something so crazy! She was joking, of course, but she said she was pretty sure she'd get away with it because he was such a jerk. You never know who else saw that comedian, so I say keep your temper in control (*just in case!*).

## 6. Don't gossip about your team members, co-workers, leaders, vendors, or anyone else.

Think about it. If you're running your mouth about one team member to another employee, the one you're talking to is probably sitting there wondering what you say about them to other people. This is a surefire way to erode all trust.

## 7. Don't avoid women who work for you out of fear of harassment claims.

Treat women with respect and dignity. I'm here to tell you women need allies, not alienation. And if you're into her, but she's not into you, get over it. Don't ask her out, and don't compliment her every day. It's not the 1920s, so if she wants you, she'll do the asking. And before you do any answering, think about how it will impact your career if it goes well and if it doesn't. Which leads me to my next suggestion.

## 8. Don't show favoritism.

You might connect more easily with some team members than others. But favoritism breeds contention and resentment. Your expectations should be the same for all team members, and everyone should be treated equally. This is also one of the reasons why it's not advised to have friends or family work for you.

## 9. Don't assume your employees know anything.

Your guidelines, rules, and procedures should be crystal clear and covered often. And when you think you have said things enough times, repeat them again. Overcommunicating is not a thing. It doesn't happen.

10. Don't give your employees the inside scoop. Just don't!

Do not go to your team if you need to vent about work. Instead, seek out a colleague who can offer the guidance and advice you need. Don't put employees in this awkward position, even if they seem willing and able to listen.

11. Don't follow your team members on social media.

Since these sites are mostly intended to share personal opinions and photos, it can affect your perception of employees and feed into unconscious bias you may have. Rule of thumb: don't friend or follow. If you get requests, explain that you don't add colleagues to social media with the exception of sites that are specifically for workplace networking.

We get it. It's a delicate dance between knowing your employees and *knowing* your employees. Just realize that perfecting this balance can make a huge difference in your leadership, and more importantly, your team.

# Caring with Boundaries

If you're seeing some error in your ways and want your team members to feel like you care without crossing any boundaries, here are some suggestions:

1. The little things matter.

Send a congratulatory or encouraging email after a team win, before the holidays, or after learning about a life change. This shows that you care enough to recognize what matters to your employees outside of work—not just what they do at work.

PRO TIP

If you can't think of anything to say about your employees and their performance, this is a huge red flag. It means you don't know enough about them, and this chapter is written for you. (You're welcome!)

## 2. Make time for your employees.

Don't get so caught up in daily projects that you aren't available to chat when needed. Make it a point to have frequent conversations with your employees to show your interest and their value.

## 3. Set yourself apart as a leader.

Offer thoughtful and fun employee perks. Consider creative ideas like the following:

- offering breaks for a quick basketball game
- allowing flex time for work as long as deadlines are met
- bringing in a masseuse
- implementing a Bring-Your-Dog-to-Work Day (maybe even with mobile grooming for the pups!)
- organizing outdoor adventures as a team

Also, just about everyone loves food--how about a Taco Truck in the parking lot once a month? Any creative efforts like this show your caring nature. It demonstrates that you're invested in your employees and their satisfaction.

For your remote team, host watch parties. Send your remote team members a gift card to cover their popcorn and candy costs. Have frequent check-ins using their preferred communication method.

That way, they feel part of the team, and they can enjoy everything right along with the rest of the group.

## 4. Show an interest in spouses or significant others.

Hey! Not in that way! Stay with me. Employee performance goes up when they have support at home, so appreciating the partners behind the scenes goes a long way in showing you care. After all, work is just a fraction of a person's life.

## 5. Relate to them.

Don't brag about first-class flights, your new Porsche, or your covered parking spot. Showing your vulnerabilities and imperfections as a human being can help build a bridge between you and your team members.

Taking the time to inquire about your employees and their loved ones leads to a thriving company culture. It's a bulletproof way to connect with your team members and get to know them on a more personal level.

Think about doing some of these best practices when getting to know your employees and showing appreciation: challenge yourself to learn something new about an employee every day. Welcome new team members personally. Invite several team members at a time for lunch, keep track so that you don't leave anyone out. Work alongside your employees. Thank them on your company's social media pages. Bring back the old-fashioned Wall of Fame. Set up a suggestion box. Offer free swag. Attend work gatherings. Hold town hall meetings

Just start anywhere and adjust as you go, but never forget the human aspect. You aren't managing robots.

# Bringing It All Together

This chapter has challenged you to consider many issues related to getting to know your employees. By knowing more about your team, you can personalize individual connections and recognition.

Additionally, being there for your employees during huge life changes is not just important; it is necessary. Like when I lost my mom, your total disregard is personally devastating to your employees. You'll appear heartless and aloof, a very bad combination for a leader. Show up and show empathy.

After stressing the importance of knowing your people, I introduced boundaries in a professional environment to help you understand what it looks like to stay in the perimeter of an invested leader without being inappropriate.

To be absolutely clear, with no chance of misinterpretation, I provided DON'Ts that will protect you and your employees. You've now seen what managers should not do with their team members.

We also looked at what you can do to show interest and concern while honoring boundaries. This chapter is overflowing with facts to keep you out of trouble while displaying your human side. Trust me, your employees need to see it!

# Self-Reflection & Solutions

It's that time again, where you take a deep breath and evaluate your performance as a manager in these areas:

- *How much time have you put into getting to know everyone on your team as a person?*
- *How many people on your team have children?*
- *What are their names?*
- *What is the employee's spouse or significant other's name?*
- *How far down in the organization can you correctly name each person?*

With those questions in mind, it's time to embrace the idea of learning more about your team members.

---

**TIP 1**

Find out what motivates each individual on your team and how they want to be rewarded.

---

You should know what gets all your direct reports out of bed each morning. Other than the mission of the organization, what matters to them most? Money, relationships, creativity?

When it comes to recognition, some people prefer a private thank you, while others want a party. Some people appreciate cash as a thank you for a job well done, while others would value a spa day. These are things you should know and track.

If your Human Resources Information System (HRIS) can't track this, I recommend doing two things:

1. Find a new HRIS.
2. Find a way to track it until you have your new system up and running. Here is a simple spreadsheet you can use as a starting point.

*https://searscoaching.com/wp-content/uploads/2019/04/Employee-Tracker.xlsx*

## TIP 2

Ask personal questions.

If you aren't sure where to begin or asking your employees questions about their personal lives doesn't come naturally to you, here are some questions for you to get to know your team members:

- *What was your first real job?*
- *What types of TV programs do you binge-watch?*
- *What do you value in a working environment?*
- *What excites you about your job?*
- *Who are your mentors?*
- *Do you enjoy traveling?*
- *What's your favorite book?*
- *Do you speak other languages?*
- *Are you taking a vacation this year?*
- *Would you say you're an introvert or extrovert?*
- *How would you describe a perfect day?*
- *How do you like to celebrate a job well done?*
- *How are we doing with collaboration at work?*

You could also create a questionnaire for employees to gain a big-picture understanding of your team members.

Even if you're not aware of them, you have biases. We all do. Though your biases may be primarily subconscious, they still can have a detrimental effect on your employees, who think you just don't care--or worse, that you're judging them.

**TIP 3**

Learn your own biases.

Here are some examples:

- **Stereotypes** are assumptions or opinions about a class of individuals who share a certain trait. Managers are no exception, and they should be careful not to let stereotypes affect their behavior. Honestly, this is an easy one to recognize. You know what I'm talking about. For example, you should make sure you don't *assume* your Asian employee is good at math or a single mother will call in sick or be late all the time. Check yourself about stereotypes and the related behavior. And then get rid of them once and for all.

ME: I'M SICK
BOSS: AND?
ME: OMW

- **Selective perception** means a manager pays attention to only some of the available information available or just information they care about. For example, if a certain employee often behaves negatively, the manager is more likely to notice the negative behavior than any positive behavior the employee exhibits. This is an unfortunate consequence that comes from selective perception. It can be remedied by making sure you note good *and* bad things about your team members.

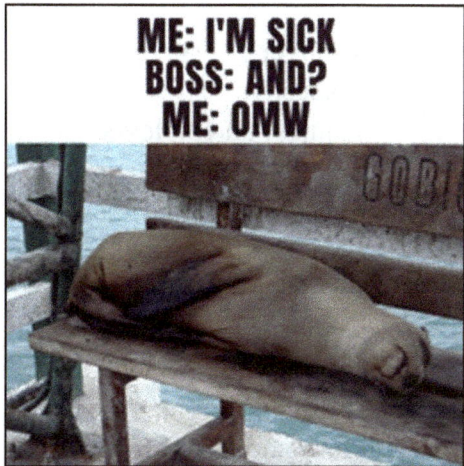

41

- **First impression bias** refers to a manager giving too much credence to their first impression of an employee. An initial judgment based on minimal facts can shape how a manager views future evidence about an employee. For instance, an employee who absolutely killed their first interview may be considered more capable than they are. The first impression affects the manager's thinking. Sometimes people think this is the "gut feeling" that allows them to be great at reading people. Not true-- this is a bias, which then feeds into other biases. You don't have a gut feeling. What you have is a bias.

- **Spillover bias** operates in the opposite way. A manager's perspective can be skewed by considering past information. For example, an employee who had wild success on a previous project may always be thought of in terms of that success by their manager, even if everything they touched for the last three years turned to poop. If you are touching base with your employees about their work and determining if they are meeting expectations on at least a quarterly basis, you can easily avoid this one.

- **Confirmation bias** means that once a decision is made, we look for information confirming our decision and ignore information that goes against our decision. For example, let's say you do an internet search asking, "Are unions bad?" All the information that shows up will say unions are bad. Keep confirmation bias in mind as a manager.

- **Negativity bias** refers to dwelling on more negative information than positive. For instance, a manager who receives a positive review overall but with some comments about needed improvements may fixate on the negative. This is sometimes a problem that comes up during 360 Leadership Assessments. Hopefully, when you do one, you have a coach who can get you unstuck and point you in the direction of growth.

- **Ingroup bias** explains how a manager might show favoritism to those in their "in" circle. A manager may show leniency to someone of his ethnicity but be harsh on someone from a different culture. This goes back to not showing favorites. Keep track of who you find yourself spending more time with and make sure you're being fair across the board.

We're talking about biases in a chapter about caring about employees because biases can affect how and if you connect with your employees. And likely, you won't even realize the impact when it's happening. Hopefully, armed with this information, you're now ready to recognize your shortcomings and step out of your comfort zone to get to know your employees as the unique individuals they are.

Now, you can better connect with your team and others in your life. Eliminating biases as a manager is as simple as learning which ones you possess, considering which ones affect you most, and determining how that impacts your company. From there, you should modernize how you hire, including referring to data and valuing diversity. Also, you can invite team members to speak up about biases.

Remember this quote from Aristotle. "The roots of education are bitter, but the fruit is sweet." Once you know better, you do better.

# HOW TO TELL IF YOU'RE AN A**HOLE BOSS

# YOUR EMPLOYEES SEEM PISSED OFF ALL THE TIME FOR NO REASON

Do you arrive with a smile but are met with angry faces? Do you work hard to put together a productive meeting, only to have it end with grumpy and irritable employees?

You've been puttering away, trying to make sure you're doing all of the rah-rah things you know helps make teams happy.

You also make sure you don't micromanage.

You give your employees tons of rope. You tell them to figure things out on their own, and for the most part, they do.

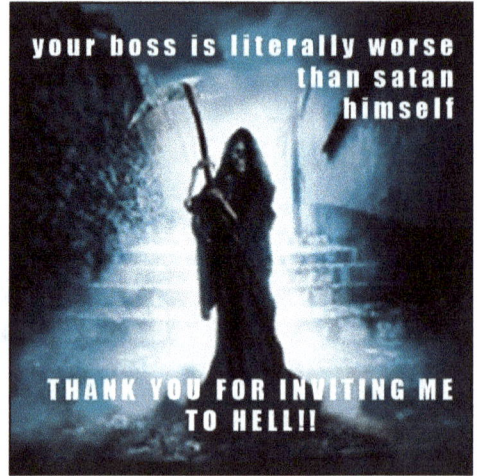

your boss is literally worse than satan himself

THANK YOU FOR INVITING ME TO HELL!!

When they need guidance, you give them a general idea and send them on their way.

But for some reason, despite all your efforts, your team still isn't bursting with happy campers. They grumble, they complain, and they still aren't working well together. In fact, they act pissed off.

All the time.

Okay, fine. You tend to instruct your team to do things without a lot of direction. You have been accused of asking people to look for a purple squirrel every now and then, but who hasn't?

And yeah, there might be some people who aren't pulling their weight, but you're pretty sure the team doesn't mind picking up the slack. When other employees complain about those lazy workers, you remind them they're part of the team and need to get along.

Let me give you an example.

## Meet Tiffany

I provided HR coverage for a leader who had a lot of these same problems. We'll call her Tiffany. She came to me unable to figure out what was wrong with her team, desperately seeking direction. She felt like she was doing all the right things, but the results were the opposite of what she was trying to achieve. Her team just was not performing.

I quickly realized that Tiffany would give the team direction, but she neglected to provide specifics on what to do. She worked that way because she had heard that telling someone what to do was terrible leadership behavior. She was also slow with performance management because she was told these plans were only used to get people out of the door.

Unfortunately, all this was bad news from her team's perspective because they found Tiffany completely disconnected. Though her intentions were good, the outcomes weren't.

Her employees had a general idea of what they should be doing, but they had zero understanding of *why* they were doing it, *when* the deadlines were, and *what* the guidelines were.

And from her employees' point of view, it was like they were being asked to do something not just tricky but completely unachievable. And guess what? *It was.*

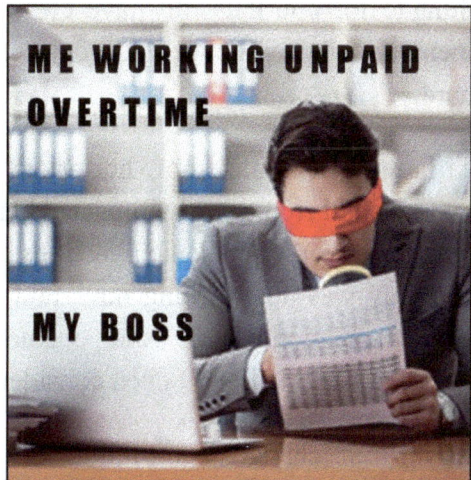

There is a lot of room between giving too much direction, also known as micromanaging, and not giving enough guidance to even get started. Unfortunately for this manager's employees, this was the leadership style she offered. The level of frustration her team experienced, as a result, caused many, many frowns.

As you know, employees' frowns are not good. And they lead to terrible outcomes.

All this doesn't even really take into account the team members who still gave a hoot. I mean, there were only a few, but they were still trying. Except they were treated the same as their peers who had clearly given up, checked out, and turned into poor performers.

Those poor, hard-working souls were receiving the exact same level of treatment at work as others who were doing significantly worse (and less).

Really, can you think of anything more demotivating?

To make this point clear, let's give an exaggerated example. Imagine you're running a sales team. Every person gets $5,000 in commission each week, no matter what they close or how they perform.

Now, typically, a few people will still work hard and feel like it's the right thing to do. You'll usually have a few of those, but mostly, you'll have team members who will check out, enjoy that direct deposit, and stop working hard.

Tiffany didn't realize how her prior "leadership training" and the mindset that evolved from it truly impacted her team. The advice she was following may have worked in some situations and at some point in time. But it most certainly was not working now, and instead of trying new strategies, she just went plowing ahead. And you know what? She didn't think her methods were wrong. She hadn't even considered it!

Look, time changes everything, and methods that worked ten years ago don't work so well anymore. Heck, some things that worked in 2019 don't work anymore! But Tiffany didn't know it and hadn't done the work to determine why her leadership style wasn't jiving with her employees.

To be clear, I don't expect this to be an ageless book of information that withstands the test of time. Nothing should. Companies, leaders, employees, and people all need to grow, or they become stagnant. Keeping up with the latest and greatest ways to make sure your team is motivated and happy is critical.

# Why Your Employees Might Be Pissed-Off

Sometimes, you let your employees leave early on Friday. You might allow them to take an extra 30 minutes for lunch after hitting a goal. You've even let them make up missed time over the weekend instead of using PTO.

But they're still mad. All the time. *What gives?*

If you are a lousy manager with angry employees, some (or all) of the following might be happening:

- You don't trust your employees.
- You are insecure in your leadership position.
- You make your employees feel anxious in their positions.
- You lead through intimidation.
- You make employees feel unworthy.
- You don't care about employee contributions.
- You make employee jobs more challenging by miscommunicating.

And if you can read that list objectively, can't you see why someone would be mad?

With this realization, let's take a closer look at what bad bosses do and don't do. If you want to stop having pissed off employees, these are some helpful dos and don'ts to start.

## 1. Bad bosses don't prepare their employees for challenges.

I mean, you're not a babysitter, right? In all probability, this isn't their first job, so they need to figure it out. Well, let me ask you this. *How's that working for you?* Because if they're angry all the time, it's not effective.

## 2. Bad bosses don't give their employees respect.

Just like any healthy relationship, consideration is necessary. If you're disrespecting your employees and expecting them to continue giving 110%, these are huge red flags. If you acted that way to your own boss, significant other, or parent, tell me how it would fly. It's no different at work! You can be the boss without being disrespectful. If you continue being disrespectful, is it any wonder your employees are pissed off?

## 3. Bad bosses don't trust, and therefore, they micromanage.

When you act like this, you're no longer a manager. You're a private investigator. If you can't give your employees space to do their jobs--and do so independently--you have a control problem, not an employee problem. I understand there will be employees you have to stay on to get their work done, but micromanaging isn't the answer. And for employees who do get their job done (but you still micromanage), I'll be honest--you're destroying them mentally, and you will *never, ever* tap into the best work they can do for you and the company. A healthy work environment releases responsibility so your employees can gain the experience and confidence needed to do their job well. And if you don't give them trust and independence, they're probably going to be pissed off. And they have every right to be.

## 4. Bad bosses don't understand their employee's jobs.

You're the boss. You need to know the roles of your team members. Let me say that again. You need to know the roles of your team members! If you don't, how are they supposed to follow your leadership? In addition, do you seem unhelpful or lost half the time? Who's in charge here, anyway? Get out the flow chart, check out who has what account, and understand the roles of your team. If you keep getting it wrong or acting clueless, your employees will eventually be pissed off. And can you blame them? Without employees, you're out of a job. Angry employees aren't much better. You need to figure this out by learning their responsibilities and appreciating their contributions. Keep in mind that I did not say you have to know how to do your team members' jobs. You can lead a team of software engineers without knowing how to be a software engineer, but you have to know what a software engineer *does*. Got it?

## 5. Bad bosses don't reward a job well done, which is a big problem.

If employee morale is low, you usually have one person to blame: yourself. If you can't show appreciation for your team's work and accomplishments, they're going to be pissed off. No question. Would you work hard for someone who never said *"thank you"* or *"well done?"* I'll answer that; you wouldn't. If you aren't already praising and rewarding your workers, you need to start. And you need to keep it up. Consistently. Doing so motivates your team to work harder. Not doing so pisses them off.

## 6. Bad bosses don't show employee loyalty.

Your team is there for you, so you need to be there for your employees. If you do things like blame your employees for mistakes or deny time off for the person who has been with you for ten years because you want the day off, you better expect two consequences: (1) you're unprofessional, so you're setting the tone and making that behavior acceptable, and (2) it reflects badly on you, and your employees will let you know through their actions, if not their words. You've blown up trust with PURE DYNAMITE. I mean, you went big and destroyed any loyalty they had. If you're going to be the boss, you better figure out how to make suggestions to solve problems, not point fingers. If you aren't loyal to your employees, they'll be pissed off. Period.

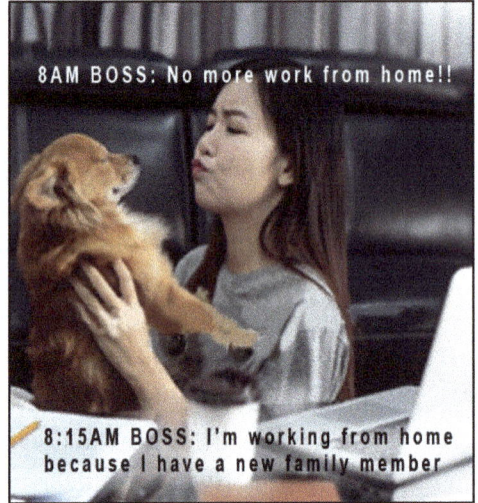

8AM BOSS: No more work from home!!

8:15AM BOSS: I'm working from home because I have a new family member

Now that we've considered some mistakes you may or may not have made as a manager, let's look at how you can change your leadership behavior. Typically, there are six stages you'll pass through as you seek to make any type of modification, whether personally or professionally.

Come along with me for this critical lesson so you can get moving in the most productive direction as a manager and un-anger your team members.

# Changing Your Behavior as a Leader

We've already established that you're doing one or two things wrong with your pissed-off employees. After all, content employees don't usually feel overwhelmingly irate on a regular basis.

Since you've determined you need to transform your leadership style, let me point you to the mindset required for lasting change. Research says initiating *any* change requires the proper state of mind. And like the great Maya Angelou said, "If you don't like something, change it."

Whether you want to stop smoking, start saving money, lose weight, or become a better manager, you must alter your behavior.

With this in mind, allow me to walk you through the six stages people move through when making significant changes. Before you can make any type of progress, you'll need to determine where to begin altering your leadership style.

### 1. Pre-contemplation.

The fact is that people resist change. In this stage, the individual hasn't even considered making a change. They're comfortable in their choices and behaviors, and any suggestion for change will likely be met with defensiveness. There's no intention to change.

Managers tend to spend a lot of time in this stage, mostly because they're *in charge* and no one should *question the boss*. Sound familiar? The leading feature of this stage is that ignorance is bliss. They don't realize that they are the problem.

### 2. Contemplation.

By now, a person has realized there's a problem. Their brain has sent them the message that something isn't right, and it's time to pay attention. The individual is contemplating some adjustments. They are no longer pointing fingers at others, and they are starting to take ownership of the problem and the part that they may plan in it.

People are open to feedback and suggestions in this stage, but they still need encouragement and support to get moving. They still might feel ambivalent and uncommitted. You could call this stage being on the fence, and it often lasts the longest because actually taking action can feel overwhelming.

In the contemplation stage, a manager has realized they have a problem and has decided to stop hoping for miracles. They realize by now that employees won't just walk in next Monday with a cheerful grin and helpful attitude. So now the manager is considering what needs to change in their behavior since it appears the employees aren't changing anything.

3. **Preparation.**

At this stage, there's no more denial. The person knows it's time to make a change. They're researching strategies and resources to be successful. For example, if they want to stop smoking, they might visit their doctor for help. Or, if they want to carve out more time for friends and family, they'll consider significant changes in their schedule to accomplish this. The bottom line is that the individual is preparing to take action, testing out the waters.

Many people try to skip this step and go straight to the next step, action, but they'll often fail because they don't yet have the proper knowledge to succeed.

Lesson learned? Do your homework. Experience has already taught you that cranky employees aren't any fun, nor are they productive.

4. **Action.**

This is where the rubber meets the road. Behavior changes occur with focused efforts. Transformation feels exciting, and the person is motivated to keep going. They use the proper willpower and restraint to move toward their goal.

Unfortunately, though, this is often the shortest stage. Failure is highly possible based on the individual's motivation, so they'll need to keep their eye on the prize.

It's vital to know that this stage focuses on whether *what you're doing* is working. If it's not, then what needs to happen for long-term change? Also, you'll need to realize change isn't immediate. Particularly if you're making extensive changes, you'll need to practice patience, effort, and determination to see results.

## 5. Maintenance.

The individual has reached their goal in this stage, but the truth is, it's still challenging. There was a robust, focused intensity when the person started out, but that drive has lessened. The shine has worn off, if you will.

This stage is where an individual will most likely relapse. Even though they know their goal is worthwhile and meaningful, their level of support may be reduced. A good way to help combat failure at this stage is having a mentor who's available for encouragement. Managers often fall back into their old ways if the new habits don't feel adequate. But just like all things worth accomplishing, you must continue even when the road is arduous and lengthy.

## 6. Relapse.

The fall from grace happens here. The person has reverted to their prior behavior and either lost the battle or ultimately gave up. Don't stay down! The key here is to identify the trigger that caused the relapse and be more equipped to prevent vulnerability in future efforts. Take a minute to think about what went wrong and determine how you can avoid repeating the mistake.

I realize this might sound like a lot of psychological mumbo-jumbo, but if you don't know where you are, how can you figure out where to go? Take a long, hard look at these stages--and yourself.

On what do you spend the most time? What steps can you take to be successful? What triggers and traps keep you from actual change?

Often, it can appear that people are lazy or resistant to change, but the truth is, many people just aren't familiar with these stages of change. But now you are, so you don't have an excuse for remaining in ineffective patterns. Knowledge is power, my friend. You should also know that you might cycle through these stages many times, but you can look at slip-ups as an opportunity to learn and grow.

I know you don't want to hear this, but if your employees are always pissed off, you need to make some changes. Now that you can recognize where you are and where you need to go, you're more likely to create trust, build relationships, and earn loyalty from your employees.

Circling back to Tiffany, she had several ups and downs. It took her a while to really get in the groove, she would go back to her old way of doing things without even realizing it. Then I asked her what her team knew about her leadership journey. Turns out, they didn't know that she was trying to improve her leadership skills, she was embarrassed to tell them that she didn't know everything about being a leader. I asked her to think about what she'd just said through the lens of the Tiffany who was actively trying to be a better leader.

The light bulb went off!

Of course, she filled in her team and let them know what behavior she was trying to change. Her team rallied behind her, and they made a game of it. When Tiffany's behavior reverted, she had to put $1.00 in the Train Tiffany jar. After several months, things were going a lot better. Her team felt like they rounded the corner and they surprised her by matching the money in the jar and went out for happy hour.

# Bringing It All Together

Chapter 3 felt like a bad movie there for a while, didn't it? Cranky employees with no solution in sight!

Even with your best attempts, your team is pissed off all the time. To demonstrate why this might be happening, you got to meet Tiffany, a leader who wanted direction but was paralyzed by bad advice she'd received. Her behavior as a result just caused problem after problem, particularly in the area of micromanaging.

One of Tiffany's main problems was that she didn't update her leadership style with the times. Workplaces are constantly evolving and shifting, so leaders must be willing to keep up with the needs in their corner of the world.

Like Tiffany, you might be guilty of any of the following reasons, which would be enough to piss off the nicest person alive: you don't prepare your employees for challenges, you don't give them respect, you don't trust them, and you don't show employee loyalty. Additionally, you might not even understand what their jobs are, and you sure don't reward jobs when they're well done.

On paper, this looks pretty bad. If you read it out loud, it sounds even worse. But you do have the power to change your behavior as a leader. To better prepare you for this leap, I shared the six steps you'll go through when making any kind of significant change. I encourage you to return to this information again and again until it sinks in, and you achieve lasting change.

With all this information in mind, we need to self-reflect carefully and then pursue solutions. Let's go.

# Self-Reflection & Solutions

It's that time again, where you take a deep breath and evaluate your performance as a manager:

- *What are you doing to see how well your leadership style has fared over time?*
- *What are you doing to upgrade your leadership skills?*
- *How often are you getting feedback on your leadership style?*
- *Where are you in the stages of change? Where do you need to be?*
- *How often do you ask your employees, "How are you?" and wait for a truthful response that you actually care about.*

As a leader, you should upgrade your management skills like you upgrade your smartphone. In addition, you want to self-reflect often to determine how you can improve your management skills--then take the required steps to do so. You'll need to remain committed to the process, even when it's challenging. And be sure to define your goals and desired outcomes so you can measure them. Then, be ready to improve new areas in the next go-round. Here are a few tips to get started.

You've taken a significant step by reading this book, but if you see yourself in any of these stories, you have a long road ahead of you. And that's okay. Just be aware that change doesn't happen overnight, as we've already pointed out. In fact, you'll need to extend grace to yourself in this process.

Make sure you have an accountability buddy who will help you stay on track and meet your goals.

> **TIP 1**
>
> Take the time to continue your leadership journey.

Also, have patience. As an executive coach, I don't typically see any lasting changes until roughly three or four months into an engagement. If you haven't seen change and it has been a few months, give it a few more.

One thing I always recommend for leaders is to do some training with their team. Group coaching and workshops can be fun and helpful. I have personal preferences for products to help teams learn more about their automatic behaviors and their communication and learning styles, but I won't micromanage and tell you what to use. I will say, whatever you use, make sure that it also helps people learn to be more tolerant of differences, which can help your entire team become more inclusive.

> **TIP 2**
>
> Break old habits and form new ones.

A habit is something that someone does regularly. Bad habits are typically hard to stop doing, and good habits can be difficult to start doing. especially one that's difficult to give up or implement. Habits usually occur subconsciously and take a concentrated effort to change. But if you have pissed off employees, it's time to bust out the old and break in the new.

Consider the following recommendations when implementing a new habit:

1. **Give it 90 days.**

   To make a new behavior stick, you need more than just three or four weeks for it to become automatic. There's a conditioning phase, so give yourself a solid month before expecting to see anything at all. I can't stress this enough: do not expect overnight change, or you'll be severely disappointed.

2. **Make it happen daily.**

   Implementing a new habit requires daily effort, not just a hit-and-miss approach throughout the week.

3. **Begin simply.**

   Some of us get ahead of ourselves by trying to change too much at once. When putting one new behavior into practice, focus on just that: one.

4. **Set reminders.**

   After you're 10-14 days into the new habit, it's easy to get off track. The best way to avoid failure is to set reminders that will motivate you to stay focused.

5. **Find a buddy.**

   A friend who will walk this journey with you is worth their weight in gold. They can help keep you motivated and remind you why you started in the first place on difficult days.

6. **Treat it like an experiment.**

   This doesn't mean *not* taking it seriously, but give it 90 days of honest effort before you decide to throw in the towel. If you aren't getting the results you want, it may be time to go back to the drawing board and see what needs tweaking.

## 7. Know the benefits.

Remember why you started. As you begin to notice minor improvements, you'll receive the inspiration necessary to keep going.

Remember that on average, it takes 18-24 days to create a habit and 66 days for a habit to stick. So, if you're used to doing things a certain way, it will take effort to do things differently and consistently.

**TIP:** Find different resources.

Unlike my collection of plain black leggings, there is no one-size-fits-all to improving your management style. People learn differently, and all leadership techniques don't work in all situations and company cultures.

One of the best ways to grow and develop is through on-the-job training. It can be overwhelming to pinpoint what you need to develop the proper skills for your career, but here are some common areas to focus on when seeking to increase your overall capabilities as a leader. I can promise you that effort here will pay off in happier, less frustrated employees.

| Competency | What It Includes |
|---|---|
| Deciding and initiating action | Making decisions, taking responsibility, acting with confidence, acting on your own initiative. |
| Leading and supervising | Providing direction and coordinating action, supervision and monitoring behavior, coaching, delegating, empowering staff, motivating others, developing staff, identifying and recruiting talent. |
| Working with people | Understanding others, adapting to the team, building team spirit, recognizing and rewarding contributions, listening, consulting others, communicating proactively, showing tolerance and consideration, demonstrating empathy, supporting and caring for others, developing and communicating self-knowledge and insight. |
| Adhering to principles and values | Upholding ethics and values, acting with integrity, utilizing diversity, showing social and environmental responsibility. |
| Relating and networking | Building rapport, networking, relating across levels, managing conflict, using humor. |
| Persuading and influencing | Making an impact, shaping conversations, appealing to emotions, promoting ideas, negotiating, gaining agreement, dealing with political issues. |

| Presenting and communicating information | Explaining concepts and opinions, articulating key points of an argument, presenting, public speaking, projecting credibility, responding to an audience. |
|---|---|
| Writing and reporting | Writing correctly, writing clearly and fluently, writing in an impressive and engaging style, targeting communication. |
| Applying expertise and technology | Applying and building technical expertise, sharing expertise, using technology resources, demonstrating physical and manual skills, showing cross-functional awareness, demonstrating spatial awareness. |
| Analyzing | Analyzing and evaluating information, testing assumptions and investigating, producing solutions, making judgments, demonstrating systems thinking. |
| Learning and researching | Learning quickly, gathering information, thinking quickly, encouraging and supporting organization learning. |
| Creating and innovating | Innovating, seeking, and introducing change, listening to different perspectives. |
| Formulating strategies and concepts | Thinking broadly, approaching work strategically, setting and developing strategy, visioning. |
| Planning and organizing | Innovating, seeking, and introducing change, listening to different perspectives. |

| | |
|---|---|
| **Developing results and meeting customer expectations** | Focusing on customer need and satisfaction, setting high standards for quality, monitoring and maintaining quality, working systematically, maintaining quality processes, maintaining productivity levels, driving projects to results. |
| **Following instructions and procedures** | Following directions and procedures, timekeeping and attending, demonstrating commitments, showing awareness of safety issues, complying with legal obligations. |
| **Adapting and responding to change** | Adapting, accepting new ideas, adapting your interpersonal style, showing cross-cultural awareness, dealing with ambiguity. |
| **Coping with pressure and setbacks** | Coping with pressure, showing emotional self-control, balancing work and personal life, maintaining a positive outlook, handling criticism. |
| **Achieving personal work goals and objectives** | Achieving objectives, working energetically and enthusiastically, pursuing self-development, demonstrating ambition. |
| **Entrepreneurial and commercial thinking** | Monitoring markets and competitors, identifying business opportunities, demonstrating financial awareness, controlling costs, keeping aware of organizational issues. |
| **Strategic risk-taking** | Calculating risks appropriately and making decisions that have a positive downstream impact. |

| | |
|---|---|
| **Project management** | Allocating the correct resources, financial, people, supplies, etc. and guiding teams to take a project from start to finish. |
| **Understanding P&L** | Understanding the profits and losses of the organization and your department and using the data to make strategic financial decisions |
| **Conflict management** | Resolving problems between yourself and others in a way that allows all parties to be respected and heard |
| **Strategic planning** | Determining where your organization is, where it needs to be, and putting together a plan to get there. |
| **Team building** | Participating in activities to motivate, develop, and get to know a team. |
| **Critical thinking** | Using facts to analyze data and use evidence to make unbiased decisions. |
| **Change management** | Making changes more effectively and efficiently. |
| **Coaching** | Using inquiry to help someone change behavior, perspective, and direction. |

As you can see, there are multiple avenues for improvement. You are not stuck as an *asshole boss*. You have all the resources needed to implement lasting change and build employee relationships.

Happy employees aren't pissed off. Get them happy and keep them happy. It's vital to realize that a great deal of their attitude is within your control.

For more ideas, direction, and information, check out the following link:
*https://searscoaching.com/on-the-job-learning-activities/*

# YOUR PRODUCTIVITY IS WAY DOWN

*Are your numbers bad? Like really bad? And even though you've tried everything, your employees just suck. Or do they?*

Understandably, as a high-performing manager, you expect to have a high-performing team. Typically, your people fall in line and do what they're told. But for some reason, it's not working.

Here's an example of low productivity. Imagine you just got a new team, and things aren't going well. Everyone on the team is present every day, but based on the numbers, it seems like they're sitting around and twiddling their thumbs. Or worse, job searching during company hours.

Of course, you're exasperated. You feel like you've barked and barked, and now you just need to bite. Hard. It's what worked for you in the past... the harder you pushed, the harder your team worked.

Yeah, there was always some turnover when you cracked down. Not everyone is cut out for it. And if you can't stand the heat, get out of the kitchen. *Amirite?*

But with all your experience, you think you know what the problem is.

## Generational Gaps

Up until now, you've always had a team of older people. They fell in line with your expectations. You didn't have to meet with them all the time and repeatedly explain what they had to do. Back then, no one gave a *shit* about the vision of the organization. You don't think that really matters, anyway. I mean, since people are here to do a job, they should just do it.

Now, though, you have to deal with *The Millennials*. You're pretty sure they're the cause of the problem. They're so needy. And they tend to challenge authority and make demands that older generations would never have made.

| PRO TIP | While the federal legal age discrimination is focused on the higher end, age 40 and over, you should know counting someone out based on the year they were born is also the wrong thing to do. In some states, it's illegal as well. |
|---|---|

You're ready to go to HR and say you want to fire your whole team. And demand they not send you any candidates from that *damn* Gen Z.

But before marching to HR in a huff, ask yourself a couple of questions.

1. *Is everyone aware of their specific roles and responsibilities?*
2. *Is everyone aware of your expectations of them?*

Start there.

You'd be amazed by how many people, even after being in a role for years, can be working outside of the scope of their role. They could be underperforming without even realizing it.

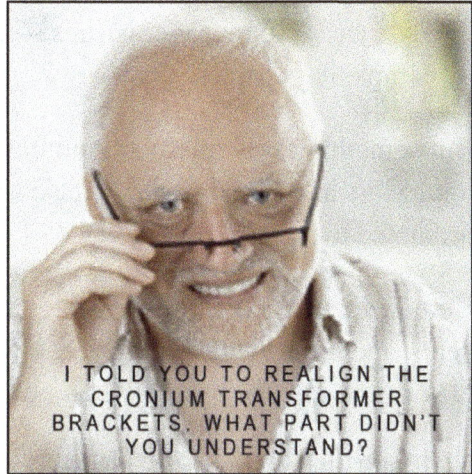

I TOLD YOU TO REALIGN THE CRONIUM TRANSFORMER BRACKETS. WHAT PART DIDN'T YOU UNDERSTAND?

Consider the above questions carefully. Now, do you remember those one-on-one meetings we talked about? Yep, it's time. Be sure to set up one-on-one sessions with your team. Set a cadence that makes sense for you to be aware of what each person is doing and where they may struggle. You'll then want to check in regularly to stay on top of what's going on and what they need from you.

Really, look around you. How many *successful* teams operate with a command-and-control style of leader? Whether you want to face it or not, your leadership directly affects productivity--both positively and negatively. Which one are you?

Storytime!

# Meet Mike

I worked with a manager named Mike, who was pretty sure the command-and-control leadership style was the way to go. He considered himself an overly successful manager because—for him—success was purely defined by completing business goals.

But something was missing. And unfortunately, it wasn't really discussed until Mike had already been at the company for over 15 years and had been promoted to a fairly high level.

Here lies the problem. While Mike's leadership style may have worked 15 years ago, it was becoming less and less effective when the company factored in how the business goals were being completed and at what cost.

This isn't uncommon. There used to be no simple way to track turnover, attrition, or engagement.

Leaders could do all sorts of things—even *bad things*—with zero accountability.

For example, people could literally be worked to death, and there would be few to no repercussions.

Oh sure, there would be stories about bad managers, but there was usually very little proof. So, for a manager, telling people what to do and getting extremely outraged when they didn't do exactly what they were told was Mike's norm. As you can imagine, productivity suffered—big time.

In fact, a manager could have a completely new team of unhappy employees every six months, but no one cared as long as the goals were met. We'll revisit this later, so keep it in the back of your mind for now.

Consider this. Moving into management and using it as an opportunity to treat people like crap was like a rite of passage for some people. It was not only expected but even *encouraged.*

And for training? It went something like this. "You paid your dues, so they should, too." People were trained to treat their adult teams like children.

And as you can imagine, it has caused *so many problems* and produced *so little productivity.*

Back to Mike. He had a team that turned over about every 18 months because he fully embraced the style of managing people in the accepted manner for many years. No one had really said anything to him. He was getting things done, and it didn't matter what dead bodies he left in his wake. He was seen as a top manager and had zero accountability.

But Mike's leadership style was fast becoming obsolete.

# Adapting and Updating Your Management Style

Take it from me. Working in HR allows someone a unique perspective. I could see things from the employee's perspective and the managers' point of view. I could understand how the manager's actions impact the employee and the company. I could predict how the employee's reaction to the manager affects their peers, the company, and the manager.

This allows someone in HR to have a clearer picture of how the manager's style of handling their team truly impacts the company and its productivity.

As a result, a good HR professional will try to help the manager improve, but if there isn't evidence that it impacts the company negatively, there may not be much company support. Essentially, this means that no one will take action and force the manager to change their style.

At this intersection, technology becomes the best friend of HR and the worst enemy of an *asshole boss*.

Unfortunately, most companies don't make changes based on the damage done by the manager's bad behavior until it directly impacts its finances. Thanks to the wonderful world of technology, we can now quickly ascertain that bad managers have a negative impact on a company's finances.

Unfortunately for Mike, I was able to figure out two things as an HR professional.

First, his behavior was causing employees to quit far more often than the employees of his peers. They stayed for about 18 months at maximum, and the cost of replacing those employees far outweighed the revenue produced by his team meeting their goals year after year.

Next, I was able to show just how much money the company lost by Mike being a jerk and telling people what to do. The bare minimum it costs to replace someone is about a week's pay, but for some positions that are more difficult to fill (ex. engineering positions), the cost might amount to the company's entire year's pay.

For Mike's team, the cost was in the hundreds of thousands annually. Let that sink in. *Hundreds of thousands.*

In this situation, the icing on the cake was the ability to tie Mike's turnover directly to the employee's behavior. People on the way out often give very unfiltered feedback. They either don't care if they burn the bridge (which they aren't) or want things to improve for the people left behind. So, doing exit interviews are critical.

I'm sure you can guess the outcome here. The exit interviews with Mike's team all had the same theme. They didn't like being told what to do with zero agency and being belittled or yelled at.

Some leaders and even HR professionals don't give credit to exit interviews, believing that employees are vindictive and mean on their way out. But I disagree. Employees may be vindictive and mean, but their opinions *absolutely* count. What did the company do to make this person vindictive and mean? Most employees don't start out that way.

Even with the controversy of exit interviews, and the idea that some are exaggerated, there are often obvious themes that come out over time during exit interviews.

So, for managers with a leadership style like Mike, when you're on a tear about things not getting done, you should look inward first.

Let me tell you why.

I'm going to say it over and over again. Most times, the problem doesn't actually sit with the team. It sits with *you*. Telling people to do better, making them work more hours, or pushing them like a plow horse simply doesn't work. Productivity suffers, and so does morale.

Remember that if you have high expectations of your team, you should expect that they have high expectations of *you*, too. Right back at *ya!* Pot calling the kettle black, anyone?

In 2019, I wrote the following:

> *As anyone who has worked in human resources for a long time can tell you, the hiring game is changing, and it's only getting harder for employers and potential employees. Once upon a time, potential employees looking for work were tasked with proving their worth to potential employers. Today, top talent comes with a list of skills as well as a list of demands. Job applicants are willing to work hard for their employers, but they expect more than a paycheck in return.*

Wow. Doesn't that ring true?

And just think, that was even before *Little Miss Rona* decided to wipe out more than four million people globally.

## Learning from the Pandemic

Friend, do not underestimate the change in sentiment that almost everyone working for you probably has now. A lot of people started working from home in 2020. As a result, people had significant lifestyle changes, and scores of people realized how unhappy they were at their jobs and left in droves. Millions and millions of people quit their jobs during the global pandemic. How awful do you have to be to have your employees up and quit during such an uncertain time?

People are literally demanding to be treated better when they are at work.

You may have been on the receiving end of a resignation, or you may have even been the one resigning. Either way, a lot has shifted. The global pandemic hit hard, and if it didn't force you to change your leadership style, I hope knowing that *you're an asshole boss* will. Let's get this fixed and improve your team's productivity in the process.

# Productivity by Generations

I don't like to make generalizations, but it may be beneficial for you to find out the generational differences of your team. Understanding the difference between someone who grew up using Instagram and someone who learned QWERTY on an electric typewriter can make a huge difference in your leadership approach. Technology has made massive changes to the way people work, so paying attention to those changes will make you a better and more connected leader.

Let's have a quick history lesson over the different generations, their influences, and their defining characteristics. After all, if you don't understand them, you can't force much productivity out of them. Your way or the highway just won't work.

| Multiple Generations at Work: Insight for Managers | | | |
|---|---|---|---|
| **Group and Birth Years** | **Formative Influences** | **Workplace Traits** | **Defining Characteristics** |
| **Traditionalists** or **Silent Generation** 1925-1944 | • World War II • Great Depression • Rationing • *"Seen and not heard"* as children • Fixed-gender roles • Nuclear families • Evening radio programs • Louis Armstrong, Harry Belafonte, Frank Sinatra, and Billie Holiday | • Worked at one company until retirement • Considered their job a privilege • Respectful • Strong work ethic • Emotionally mature • Favor top down chain of command • Technically challenged | • Conventional morals • Frugal, creative, and resourceful • *"Make do or do without"* • Disciplined • Value home ownership and financial security • Considered the wealthiest generation • Not deterred by adversity • Redefining aging • Sometimes slow to adapt |

| | | | |
|---|---|---|---|
| **Baby Boomers**<br>or<br>**Me**<br>**Generation**<br><br>**1945-1964** | • The American Dream<br>• Rise of the teenager<br>• Television<br>• Swinging 60s<br>• Vietnam War<br>• Civil Rights Movement<br>• Space exploration<br>• Woodstock<br>• The Beatles, Elvis Presley, The Rolling Stones, and Aretha Franklin | • Hardworking and competitive nature<br>• Goal-oriented<br>• Motivated by position<br>• Comfortable with hierarchies<br>• Equate authority with experience<br>• Motivated by recognition<br>• Early IT adaptors | • Idolized as youth<br>• Known as workaholics<br>• First generation to reject traditional values<br>• Value their rights<br>• More open-minded<br>• Risk takers<br>• Self-sufficient<br>• Helicopter parenting style<br>• Redefining the idea of retirement |
| **Gen X**<br>or<br>**The "Middle Child"**<br>**Generation**<br><br>**1965-1980** | • Reagan and Gorbachev<br>• AIDS epidemic<br>• Latch-key kids<br>• First PC<br>• Working parents and rising levels of divorce<br>• Legalized abortion<br>• MTV generation<br>• Madonna, Nirvana, Whitney Houston, MC Hammer, and *importantly, Tamica Sears, ME!* | • Entrepreneurial<br>• Value work/life balance<br>• Sometimes skeptical of authority<br>• Loyal to profession, not necessarily to employer<br>• Desire flexibility and hybrid work environment<br>• Work autonomously with low supervision<br>• Digital immigrants | • Practical, individualistic, and self-reliant<br>• Highly independent<br>• Critical thinkers<br>• Higher levels of education<br>• Fiscally responsible<br>• More open to collaboration<br>• Somewhat opposed to rules<br>• Disdain for bureaucracy<br>• Cynical about government |

| | | | |
|---|---|---|---|
| **Millennials** or **Gen Y** 1981-1995 | • 9/11 attack • Iraq invasion • PlayStation • Reality TV • Online dating • Immigration • Mass school shootings • Gender-role bending • Eminem, Lady Gaga, TLC, and Beyonce | • Values a flexible work structure • Challenges authority • Prefers collaboration • Gives respect once earned • Works *"with"* organizations, not *"for"* them • Requires direct input, support, and mentoring • Value growth opportunities • Advanced technologically | • Socially responsible and aware • Financially conscious • Value social rewards • Ethnically diverse • Challenge the status quo • Creative problem-solvers • Multitaskers • Physical wellness • Perceived as entitled and risk-averse |
| **Gen Z** 1996-2010 | • Mobile devices • Social media • Energy crisis • Cloud computing • Global warming • Economic downturn | • Digital natives who are projected to have the following traits: ▫ Independent ▫ Competitive ▫ Entrepreneurial ▫ Value job security | • Technoholics • Highly and often overly connected • Less team focused • Significantly concerned about student debt • Value sustainable environment |

With this information at your fingertips, you'll be better able to understand what drives each generation of workers. Even though Traditionalists have primarily aged out of the workforce, it's beneficial for you to appreciate where they came from to understand the generations that follow them. And while you may be trying to master the needs of those Millennials, don't forget Gen Z, who are right behind them and quite different.

If you don't understand the generational clashes and needs, you can bet the following will be directly affected: employee productivity, belonging, morale, and more. But you're in luck...our next tip guides you in managing different generations to grow loyalty—and all those other things.

Think about a leader who had a positive impact on you. If you are emulating them, but it isn't working, think about why that might be. There's no guarantee that what has worked in the past will continue to work.

That's because the world has changed. Drastically.

I talked earlier about the coronavirus, COVID-19, or as I like to call it, *Little Miss Rona*. I can't stress enough how much living through a global pandemic changed people's lives. After being told for years and years remote work was a no-go, all of a sudden, companies found a way to make it work. *Like frigging magic!*

Statistics say that about 40% of the US labor force began working from home in 2020 due to the pandemic. So, does that mean 40% of US leaders gaslighted the hell out of their employees for years? Suddenly, those who said there was no way remote work could happen found a way very quickly. Through this unexpected transition, companies kept going, and some of them even did better.

The corporate world opened up to people who were unable to get to and from an office on a daily basis. People who were ready to explode due to the number of microaggressions they had to endure daily felt a measure of relief. Some parents were able to slow down and spend more time with their children. Some people ditched the US entirely and are now working from home on a beach in Bali, which is, coincidentally, my dream.

And now, some managers are asking for their teams to come back to the office.

But as you can imagine, a lot of employees aren't having it.

The world has transformed, and I'm not sure it'll ever go back to pre-COVID. The workplace has bombarded people's living rooms. People have gotten used to doing conference calls in pajamas. They became accustomed to having more quality or family time. For all of the misery from 2020, I like to think there is one bright silver lining. Some people decided to have a more effortless life and made an enormous change. And now they have a better life.

How are you going to take the proper steps to move forward in a way that helps your employees continue to have a better life?

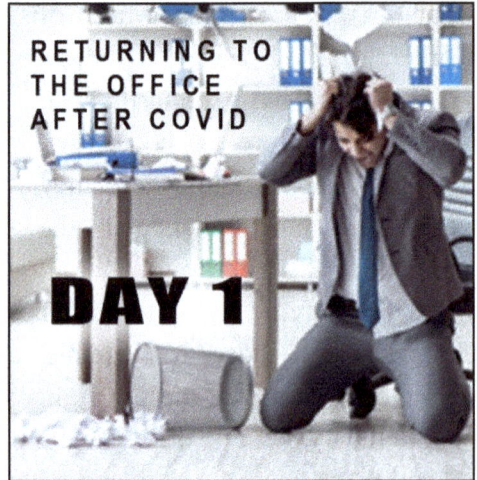

What are you willing to change so *you* can walk in the world more effortlessly?

Does it really cost you anything to be friendly and do the right thing? How much of requiring people to come back to the office is just micromanagement? Or how much of it is just being mean?

Let me share some personal insight from my experience as an employee.

# Meet Pat

I worked for someone a long time ago (we'll call this individual Pat and use a male pronoun) who went from being amiable and supportive to bitchy and mean in the blink of an eye. There was a huge tell. If Pat disagreed with my course of action or a decision I'd made, he would start his sentence with "just curious …"

From there, the conversation would deteriorate into finger-pointing, excuses, and sometimes, even tears.

It seemed like no matter my rationale, once Pat uttered those two words, there was nothing I could say that was right. It got to the point where I was just worried about when the next "just curious" inquiry would come.

Understandably, that apprehension kept me from focusing on making the right decisions, being proactive, and, in general, doing my job.

I eventually brought it up to Pat, and he told me I didn't know what I was talking about.

Then, when I let Pat know that I'd had conversations with my peers and they'd noticed the same thing, I was told to stop gossiping.

To make matters worse, when my peers were questioned to see if I'd told the truth, they all wimped out and said they hadn't noticed anything.

Over the next couple of weeks, my peers came to me privately and gave me their reasons for not telling Pat the truth. One was the breadwinner of the family and couldn't take a chance, another felt too new to the organization, etc. I heard many reasons (excuses to me) for why no one else spoke up.

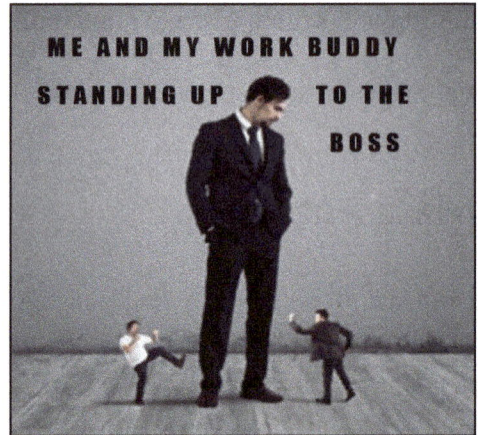

ME AND MY WORK BUDDY STANDING UP TO THE BOSS

I say this so that you understand *you hold a lot of power*.

You have the power to end someone's livelihood, make them homeless, and take away their ability to feed their children.

I think you can agree this isn't the kind of power that should be abused or mishandled.

In my case, my manager could've done so many things differently that would've had more positive results.

So, think about that employee who worked from home dutifully for over a year. And now you're asking to disrupt their life, which they struggled to build and maintain during a horrible, horrible time.

Remember, you have all the power. You certainly can drag your team back to the office kicking and screaming. You can talk down to them. But when you ask for feedback, what do you think your employees will say?

**When employees lack power, they will say what they think you want to hear, particularly if they feel the truth will harm them or their livelihood.** When you ask for feedback, and people think you won't take it well, it's unlikely that they'll tell you the truth. They may smile in your face and then start job searching. Or they might just keep getting a paycheck doing little to no work at all. That's what happens *when you're an asshole boss.*

If what you just read resonates with you, you have, in no way, created an environment that's psychologically safe enough for an open and honest conversation.

Without that, how can productivity possibly thrive? *It can't!*

With these important revelations in mind, let's look at some tips for improvement.

## Bringing It All Together

We started this chapter by looking at why your employees aren't productive. You're frustrated because you feel pushed to be a total jerk to get any results from your team.

Could it come down to something as simple as generational differences? And are those really *simple*, anyway?!

I introduced Mike as the guy who moved into management and proceeded to treat people like total crap. His attitude about "paying your dues" caused him to treat his team members like children rather than the talented, intelligent people they were.

What Mike needed desperately was a leadership makeover. HR exists for many reasons; one of them is to help leaders improve. I was one of those HR professionals for many years, and I still work with managers to help them improve their leadership style.

If the pandemic taught us anything, it's that our world has changed drastically, and that includes *how* and *where* employees work. Managers simply M-U-S-T adapt! One way to better understand what employees need is to consider managing multiple generations and how that looks. We provided a handy-dandy table to give you deep insight into the formative influences and defining characteristics of your varying team members.

Before wrapping up, I introduced you to Pat, the leader who nearly ended my career single-handedly through abuse of power.

Overall, I recommend you look closely at your leadership ideas and your employee's reactions to determine what's going on. All these factors can help you overcome reduced productivity and instead start building an atmosphere where people come first.

This is one giant step toward raising productivity and becoming a fantastic boss who left his *inner asshole attitude* in the rearview mirror.

# Self-Reflection & Solutions

Think about the first time a leader made you feel excited about going to work. Ask yourself these questions:

- *What were they like?*
- *What were you like when they were your leader?*
- *What did they do differently from what you're doing now?*
- *What has changed in you since then?*

- *When was the last time you reached out to that leader to thank them for inspiring you?*

With these questions and answers in mind, consider the following tips.

| | |
|---|---|
| **TIP 1** | Pay attention to reactions. |

When you give your team direction, pay attention to how they respond.

Then, pay attention to how you react to their response.

- *Do you find yourself getting upset with them?*
- *If they express concern, are you dismissive?*
- *Do you have a trigger or a tell that you need to start paying attention to?*

Talk to a couple of your peers and your leader to try to get feedback from them. Ask them specifically how they view your responses and reactions.

I've been through this process myself. I have a great friend who is an excellent HR Professional. She and I share a similar problem. We have very big mouths.

Now, this isn't because we are bad people or think we know everything. We just get really excited, and much like Arnold Horshack on *Welcome Back, Kotter* (*"I told y'all I'm old"*—google it if you don't get it), we just can't stop ourselves.

Once we realized this, we vowed to keep each other in check. We tried to help each other be more aware of our reactions. When possible, we'd sit next to each other and give the Eager Beaver a squeeze when our enthusiasm got the best of us.

In the same way, I recommend getting yourself an accountability partner and asking them to help you keep your reactions under control. Preferably this would be a peer, not someone on your team. As we discussed, they aren't likely to be very helpful.

Whether it's picking up your phone while someone is talking, rolling your eyes, or speaking without thinking, let someone in on what you struggle with and what to look out for. Give them permission to point out when you are reacting negatively. After some time has passed, I have a feeling you'll see productivity start to rise again.

> **TIP 2**
>
> Learn to manage different generations.

In this chapter, we introduced the unique work traits and characteristics for each generation. Using that, you can help bridge the gaps in your team by implementing the following suggestions:

### 1. Get to know your employees as individuals.

Today, inclusion and diversity are essential. By getting to know your employees as people, you can find out their values and preferences. This allows you to smash stereotyping and make everyone feel valued, leading to higher productivity.

## 2. Implement cross-generation collaboration.

Team members may naturally gravitate to workers close to their age, but different generations have a lot to teach each other. Consider setting up a mentoring program, planning team-building activities outside the work setting or creating collaborative projects. This type of teamwork increases productivity all the way around.

## 3. Find common ground.

Despite age differences, employees usually care about work that benefits everyone, affects society positively, and addresses a value or cause that everyone embraces. Find this motivating factor to bring your team together and increase results.

## 4. Understand what each group values in benefits.

Employees with young families are probably more concerned about healthcare coverage, while your tenured employees care more about retirement benefits. The reality is your workers are at different stages in life and value varying benefits. Go to bat for the diverse needs of your team—and reap the benefits with harder-working, more productive employees.

Take a minute and think about what productivity means to you. For some roles, defining productivity is really easy. For instance, if you're in sales, you probably measure how much you're selling and how much is sold by each of your team members. You most likely have a quota, and everyone knows what they need to sell to meet that mark.

> **TIP**
>
> Make sure you're measuring the right things.

But, do you take it a step further and help everyone understand how many people or companies they need to contact each day or week to meet their quotas? Do you help them learn how many prospects they need so they can contact the right number of people to meet their goals?

In other roles, it may not be as easy to determine productivity. Take Human Resources, for instance. For many people in HR, there's no such thing as a typical day. You may have a plan for your day that quickly goes awry when someone calls you or pops into your office with a concern.

With that in mind, a great way to stay on track is to have a carefully planned calendar of HR activities that your team needs to complete. This calendar should include things like succession planning, talent reviews, compensation reviews, leadership development, and compliance training.

Also, ask yourself what your HR team is doing to help the groups they support to be more productive. And are you measuring the right data to track that?

Unfortunately, the days of lazily tracking productivity based on the number of hours someone sits at their desk are long gone. And they never *really* existed as it was just something that was done because it was easy. A person sitting at their desk doesn't have anything to do with productivity. It just means they showed up that day, not that they got anything done.

When you think of measuring productivity, think about what and how an employee does that contributes to the overall goals of the company. That should be easy to do because they should have individual goals that link directly to your department's goals. In turn, those goals are inextricably linked to your company goals. *Hint, hint.*

Those goals, if done correctly, are measurable and should help you determine true productivity.

Having said that, there are some things you should avoid at all costs.

For example, with the increase in remote work, some companies track what their employees do every day. There are now companies that sell the ability for managers to get periodic snapshots taken from the employee's computer. The manager uses that to see if the employee is at their desk and working.

*This is so, so very wrong.*

I don't know how this is seen as anything other than a flagrant and disturbing violation of privacy. My advice to anyone who has a manager doing this is to run away quickly and never look back.

Think about it. As a human being, how does it make you feel to know that while you're sitting at home working, your boss can drop in and see everything you're doing? Do you feel trusted? Do you feel empowered? Do you feel like giving your everything to the person who is doing that to you?

In the end, resorting to those measures doesn't actually help determine if your employees are productive. It amounts to the same approach as making sure there are butts in chairs, which we've already established isn't helpful in the least.

I recommend you reflect on your company goals and what your team does to help the company meet those goals. When you have that solidified in your head, tracking true productivity should be a lot easier. And of course, if you don't have those goals, you can't track anything until you do, so get on it!

Armed with the knowledge from this chapter, your toolkit as a leader has just expanded greatly. Your ability to discern what matters to each generation of workers and understand your traits based on your generation will elevate your skills, success, and strength as a leader who inspires your team to be more productive and cohesive.

# YOUR EMPLOYEES CALL IN SICK ... ALL THE TIME

*You can't count on anyone to be in the office. Does flu season really last that long?*

You're patting yourself on the back for making it through COVID-19. Your team was spared, and so far, no one has tested positive. This hasn't been the case at many companies, so you're breathing in a huge sigh of relief.

For some reason, though, people keep calling in sick. Despite being fully staffed, you keep moving projects around and extending deadlines because some of your team members are out frequently.

In fact, pretty much everyone on the team has been out for at least a couple of days in the last few months.

The chances of everyone having the flu are pretty slim.

Perhaps the problem is that they're just not that into you.

A team that often calls in sick is a dead giveaway: they have a bad boss.

Now, you may disagree with that notion, but let's take this step by step.

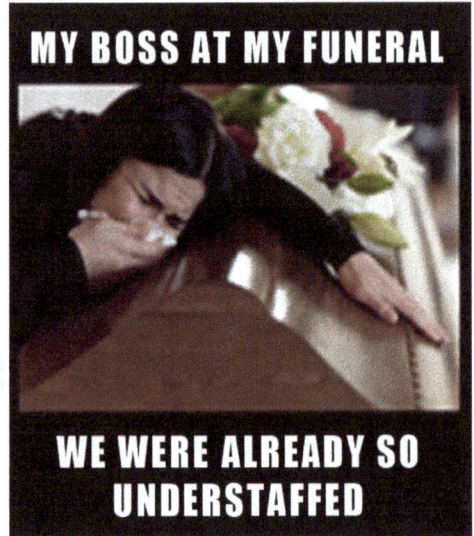

MY BOSS AT MY FUNERAL

WE WERE ALREADY SO UNDERSTAFFED

When someone calls in sick, do you ask them about how they are doing in a kind, non-obtrusive way?

Do you immediately think they're faking?

Does your mind wander towards the "we will never get this done because my employees are lazy" road?

Unless you're so much of an *asshole* that you started this book in Chapter 5, you know what's coming.

Yeah, the problem is probably you.

I guess you could be working in a *sick building* (that might be a 90s thing. I don't know if we even have any of those these days), but if people are not showing up at work regularly, you may be the cause. What's even worse is people who are working from home and *still* calling in sick.

Oh, whoops, did that hit too close to home?

*Houston, we have a problem!*

There are so many reasons, but we're going to focus on one specific reason why it's personal for me. I read an article written by Ruchika Tulshyan in *The New York Times* that talked about women of color not wanting to return to the office post-COVID.

I felt it bitterly. While I can only speak based on my own experience, a leader who fails to provide a psychologically safe environment will instead create this type of situation: *shit* rolls downhill, and, like it or not, women of color are typically at the bottom. Who in the world wants to go to work in a place like that?!

To better understand this scenario, come along with me for a moment, and put yourself in my shoes. Fair warning: *they're 4" stilettos!*

# Surface-Level Diversity

I once worked for a company that wanted to put a new focus on diversity and inclusion. One of their solutions was to create a diverse, psychologically safe environment for everyone. Their solution included creating a policy that said that there must be a diverse slate of candidates for every open position at the director level or above.

I'll tell you what this really meant: they had to have at least one woman and a person of color as part of the people being interviewed. It was like the Rooney Rule, the NFL policy stating teams must interview ethnic and minority candidates for head coaching and some senior positions.

At first, I wasn't sure where I stood on our new policy, but I quickly took a hard stance.

When the policy rolled out, my manager at the time was a complete and utter *asshole*. Instead of speaking positively about the change, he said something along the lines of "it's stupid and unnecessary because the best person for the job should get it. I don't see color."

I let him know that giving more diverse people a chance to interview for roles was the point, and when someone says, "I don't see color," it's a microaggression (or a statement of discrimination against minorities, even if indirect, unintentional, or subtle).

Then that wonderful man told me microaggressions weren't really a thing. How wonderful. They don't exist? *Please.*

Even if we'd had the best relationship in the world up to that point, his statements would have been enough for me to never trust him again. Why? Because what he said invalidated my life experiences.

A good leader understands that just because something hasn't happened to them doesn't mean it never happens.

For example, if my aunt survives cancer, but your aunt doesn't, would it make any sense for me to say *everyone* survives cancer? No, of course not. We just had different experiences. One does *not* invalidate the other or make either experience less real. Accordingly, when someone tells me my lived experiences aren't accurate, it causes a significant lack of trust both ways.

And without trust, you're screwed.

Without trust, your employees don't want to be at work.

And without trust, *you really have nothing.*

# Trust and Tact

I'm not the first leadership development self-proclaimed genius who thinks trust is the best way to start becoming a great leader. If you take the time to think about it, it's common sense. Would you follow someone you *didn't* trust? Would you follow someone you thought didn't trust *you*? Would you love being at work with someone who treated you as lesser?

The bottom line is that psychological safety is built on trust. It isn't about being "woke" or conservative or anything like that. If you start trusting your employees and their lived experiences, they will start trusting you. Having a psychologically safe environment might seem like a lot of woo, but it is vitally important.

It means you have a culture allowing people to speak freely, give ideas, admit mistakes, and trust that there won't be any negative consequences for doing so. It's difficult to do, but what thing worth doing is easy? Building trust is key.

**MONDAY**

also tuesday wednesday thursday friday

I'm here to tell you that it's the only way to start building better relationships.

What does this have to do with calling out sick, you ask?

Well, when I had that awful manager who said microaggressions don't exist, what he didn't understand was that to me, it felt like he told me it's okay for people to touch my hair. It's okay for people to assume I work for someone on my team instead of the other way around.

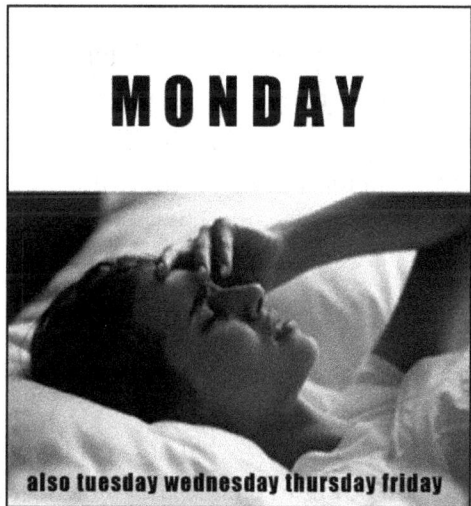

And it's okay to ask me over, and over what my ethnicity is or cheerfully tell me I don't sound Black.

In actuality, those are all microaggressions, and none of them are okay.

One tells me I am "other," and for some reason I'll never understand, it's OK to pet me at work. One assumes I'm not a leader of a team. One is rude and makes it seem like somehow true ethnicity isn't good enough. And one insinuates that, somehow, sounding *not Black* is a good thing, which would make sounding Black a bad thing.

This brings me back to my original point. Why would I subject myself to being told every day that my natural state of being was somehow negative? Why would I want to be in this type of atmosphere?

So, after my boss and I had that conversation, I was out sick a lot. This isn't a huge surprise, people. And it happens all the time.

It just didn't feel good to interact with someone who didn't trust me and who I most certainly did not trust. What would it have cost that manager to take a minute to truly listen and believe that I was giving an accurate representation of my work experience?

Nothing, really.

You probably have people on your team who don't look like you, didn't grow up in the same place as you, and don't sound like you.

With that in mind, what are you doing to make sure they feel trusted? What are you doing to ensure they know you trust them?

In other words, how are you building true relationships with your team?

I know some of these conversations are hard, but they are definitely less awkward when someone comes from a genuine place. When they come from an authentic place, and you have an open mind, they may even change the course of your relationship with your team.

It's true that sometimes, people have pretty heavy things going on at home. I've worked with people who have sick spouses and children. Those are really complex situations to manage, and when people are trying to cope with challenges like that, they need time off of work.

What they *don't* need is some *asshole* giving them a hard time about how much time they are spending with sick family members. Yes, I know the work needs to get done. We all know. But how about putting yourself in their shoes?

Ask yourself this: *Would I rather go to work and worry all day or spend time with my sick significant other?*

Isn't the answer pretty straightforward?

# Bringing It All Together

In this chapter, we examined why your employees tend to call in sick. For some reason, it feels like more absences than other leaders deal with, and though we considered many potential reasons for this odd phenomenon, it boils down to this: it has a lot to do with your leadership style.

To improve employee attendance, I made several suggestions. For one thing, make sure that you don't just talk about diversity but actually embrace it. It is also important that you think about diversity as more than just black and white. Seriously. Diversity includes religion, marital status, parental status, neurodiversity, language/accent, socioeconomic status, age and so many other things, Next, it's vital to lead with trust and tact to create a psychologically safe environment. In doing so, you'll eliminate microaggressions and be open to difficult conversations about how you can improve when needed. Finally, try to be more understanding when employees have difficulties at home, like caring for an ill family member.

All in all, this chapter serves to identify why your employees might be hiding behind an excuse of illness when the real reason is their lack of trust and confidence in you as a leader. With this in mind, let's turn our attention to reflecting on your leadership up to now and what solutions exist to help you do better.

# Self-Reflection & Solutions

It's your favorite time. Time to reflect on what you just read and consider your own leadership approach:

- *How are you tracking time off?*
- *Are people really always calling in sick, or is that just your perception?*
- *If people call in sick more than you think they should, what are you doing to understand why?*
- *Are people ill?*
- *Do they have to take care of other people?*

If you don't know this, it's a problem. You may not know the nitty-gritty details. And that's okay. But you *should* know if someone is really sick, even if it is just to encourage them to stay out of the office and get well.

Before you make any decisions, make sure you have all the facts.

TIP 1

Get your facts straight.

For example, is the employee you're approaching on protected leave? You must look into this *before* taking action. I'm not a lawyer and not a huge fan of saying whether things are legal or illegal, but keep this in mind: most times, doing the moral or right thing will keep you in the legal column. Messing around with someone's protected leave can land you in serious hot water, so watch your P's and Q's.

Check with your Human Resources department or your legal team before you go any further. And remember, no one owes you an explanation for why an employee is sick or what's wrong. Honestly, that's none of your business.

I don't really like the compliance parts of HR, but sometimes you have to pay attention to them. In this case, federal and state laws ensure a mandatory leave of absence for certain employees. Not everyone has to comply, so there are factors to consider, like how many employees a company has and where the employee works. But because many companies have to comply with certain regulations, let's take a quick look at FMLA and ADA.

The **Family Medical Leave Act (FMLA)** gives employees an unpaid leave of 12 weeks, guaranteed, without a threat of job loss, for issues like:

- bonding with a new baby through birth, adoption, or foster care
- dealing with a serious illness yourself
- caring for a family member with a major health condition
- handling a serious issue associated with an active-duty military family member

To qualify for FMLA, an employee must have worked at least 1,250 hours in the 12 months prior. Generally, the business must also have over fifty employees.

The **Americans with Disabilities Act (ADA)** requires legal compliance for qualified workers who need accommodations, ensuring no unfair discrimination against employees. The ADA applies to all elements of employment, including job application procedures, hiring and firing, compensation, training, advancement, and benefits. This act also covers advertising, recruitment, layoffs, and tenure.

- **Physical impairments** are physiological conditions or disorders, anatomical loss, or cosmetic disfigurement that impact any of the following systems:
    - musculoskeletal
    - neurological
    - cardiovascular
    - digestive
    - reproductive
    - respiratory
    - endocrine
    - hemic and lymphatic
    - skin
    - genitourinary
    - special-sense organs

- **Mental impairments** include psychological disorders like mental or emotional illness, mental retardation, organic brain syndrome, and learning disabilities.

On a federal level, beyond these laws, voluntary leaves are not guaranteed by law and are based on company policy. There are, however, many states with other leave laws you'll want to look into before coming down hard on someone for their attendance.

Otherwise, there are a few things to avoid when it comes to employees and protected leave. Though your HR department likely has this covered, it won't hurt to refresh you on the basics:

1. **Do not permit 100% healed policies.**

   Rules requiring workers to be completely healed before coming back to work violate the ADA. Even if an employee isn't entirely healed, they could return to work with accommodation. And working from home is considered a reasonable accommodation.

2. **Do not permit no-fault leave policies.**

   Another violation of ADA occurs when workers are terminated for exceeding a preset amount of leave. Again, the employee may be able to return to work with accommodation.

3. **Do limit requests for medical information from the employee.**

   Only the information confirming a medical condition or impairment is necessary. Asking for more can violate the ADA.

4. **Do remember pregnancy could be covered under ADA and FMLA.**

   While pregnancy is typically covered under FMLA, pregnancy is not a disability, but some pregnancy-related conditions like gestational diabetes, anemia, or cervical insufficiency, might be. Pregnant workers with these issues may have a right to additional accommodations and you can't discriminate against someone who is pregnant so this can be a tricky one.

> **PRO TIP**
>
> Be very careful when you have a pregnant employee. As someone who has been pregnant, I can attest to 'pregnancy brain' being a real thing. Don't be the asshole boss that fires a pregnant woman three weeks before her due date. Yeah, that happened!

## 5. Do make sure that obvious and non-obvious disabilities are treated the same.

Even though you can't see depression or PTSD, both should be treated the same way as impairments you can see, like muscular dystrophy and cerebral palsy.

Unfortunately, there will always be employees who abuse a leave policy. That's what we're trying to determine in this chapter. Are they avoiding you? If they are, keep reading.

> **TIP 2**
>
> Figure out if it's you makeing the employees sick.

This one is a little trickier. I mean, you can't just schedule a meeting with the subject of *why don't you like me?*

Typically, if you've set an employee off, you have an idea of what you did. If you don't know, here's how to try to figure it out.

Imagine you've spent the last several weeks or months with this particular employee.

Now, take the time to reflect on the conversations you've had and the times this person has been out. Are there any connections there? Is this person calling in sick after talking to you? Or are they calling in sick to *avoid* talking to you?

If you genuinely can't figure it out, it's time to assume it's *you*.

At this point, it's on you to carefully work on rebuilding that relationship.

It isn't going to happen overnight, and you have to assume there will be employee behaviors that make you sad, mad or some other sort of emotion in the meantime.

Remember, those emotions are *yours* and *yours alone*.

To make myself perfectly clear, putting your emotions onto someone else is an irresponsible, inconsiderate, and *asshole* move. With that in mind, get yourself together if you *want* your team to want to be at work.

We talked little bit about doing a Leadership 360 Assessment earlier. If you want a quick and easy way to figure out if *you're* the problem, this may be the solution. The key, though, is to make sure you are committed to understanding and living with the results.

I did a 360 Assessment once for a leader, and the results were pretty unflattering. This guy that we'll call Brian thought he was highly self-aware. The results of his 360, however, showed the opposite. It pointed out that self-awareness was one of the weakest parts of his leadership.

And as we continued along, anything he disagreed with, he dismissed.

I try to remind leaders as they go through their results that what they're seeing is what they're perceived as. It isn't a condemnation of who they are as a person. This is an essential distinction because changing personality is a lot more complicated than changing the behaviors that have caused a negative perception.

Brian had a great deal of work to do. His employees didn't fully trust him. They felt like he wasn't vulnerable, approachable, or empathetic. While the team felt like he was somewhat personable, they also said he was personable in a selective way and played favorites.

These are all things I felt were completely fixable. Nothing would change overnight, but with a good action plan and a high level of accountability, I firmly believed a follow-up 360 a year later with Brian would show tremendous positive movement.

When I told Brian this, he said that even though he appreciated the process and found the feedback valuable, he wasn't willing to move forward to create and implement a plan for change. He felt the feedback was too harsh and claimed most people didn't feel that way about him. He said they just hadn't taken the time to get to know him. He took the report, and as far as I know, he never looked at it again.

A year later, instead of positive movement, he had a 75% turnover rate. *Oops!*

when you've been telling your boss about a problem for months then it finally hits the fan

As you can see, this lack of humility on the manager's part is costly, and most of the time, completely preventable.

Allowing people to help you, listening to feedback, and making appropriate changes constitute significant parts of any leader's job. Embrace them.

> **TIP**
>
> Gather real data.

Sending out anonymous surveys is typically the number one way to gather data, but I want you to think bigger than that. With a survey, you create a list of questions for employees to answer, but you probably need a more dynamic approach. Having conversations with the team, in person or virtually, will most likely yield better results.

That being said, if you truly have created a toxic work environment and your team does not feel psychologically safe, the last person they will tell is you.

I've said it time and time again: you hold a lot of power, and not everyone is going to be comfortable telling you the truth when the truth is fairly negative. If you have tried to find out what is truly going on, but you haven't been able to get the truth, it may be time to ask for help.

Start with your HR team. If they have done the work and created relationships with your employees, they may be able to get them to talk about what's really bothering them, even if it's you. If HR hasn't been successful, suggest getting outside help.

If hiring a consultant seems like a last-ditch effort to you, then you probably need one. A consultant has an outside perspective that might be just the ticket to figure out what is really going on with your team.

Additionally, outside consultants are like Switzerland, they aren't taking sides. If they do things the right way, your team will feel comfortable confiding in a neutral third party and giving enough information to help diagnose the real issue. Consultants should be able to get you real, accurate data that will help you with your decision-making.

# YOUR EMPLOYEE TURNOVER CONTINUES TO INCREASE

*Even when you make a great hire, they don't stay long. Why doesn't anyone want to work for you?*

Good HR teams go through many hoops trying to get the best candidates in front of hiring managers. Posting jobs, screening resumes, doing interviews, just to name a few. There are automated systems that reach out to passive candidates. The talent acquisition process has come a long way, but it is still exceedingly difficult to attract top talent. Even more so with "the Great Resignation" afoot.

Thus, when a manager continues to have to recruit for the same roles over and over again, red flags begin to spring up everywhere.

We talked earlier about Mike and his command-and-control management style that caused people on his team to leave very quickly. That's one of many reasons why your team wants to move on so quickly.

# Reasons for Employee Turnover

When employee engagement is low, for whatever reason, then turnover is usually high. It might be voluntary when employees leave for personal reasons or involuntary when they are dismissed due to their poor performance. It makes sense, then, that voluntary turnover is the focus to lower the overall turnover rate since good leaders have lower involuntary turnover rates. *Hint, hint.*

Employees leaving their jobs impacts the entire organization. Productivity can suffer, as can morale.

Numerous reasons exist for employee turnover. Perhaps the training quality in your organization is low or even non-existent. Due to ever-evolving technology, your employees need the training to stay relevant and knowledgeable. In turn, this improves the quality of their work and increases their productivity. Without that, employees feel like they aren't given all the tools to do the job.

It could be your organization doesn't offer real opportunities to grow. If employees can't build on their strengths and expand their knowledge, they won't stick around to do what they're good at. You can remedy this by tapping into high-potential employees who would benefit from more development and resources. These types of employees can be tremendous assets if you determine how to retain and motivate them. The bottom line is that internal mobility is incredibly valuable.

Maybe there's an inefficient hiring process in your company, a strategic element often overlooked. There's usually a need to fill vacant positions quickly, but perhaps you don't have the right processes or tools to quickly hire the best and brightest candidates. with the right groundwork. By streamlining this approach, you can hire faster and better, improving employee retention.

You could even have a workplace culture problem. In today's world, this is a no-go. In fact, 40% of employees leave because they experienced mistreatment or unfairness related to their identity. You simply cannot afford to ignore the changes going on in the workplace. As a leader, you must be open to *all employees* regardless of their ethnicity, gender, age, sexuality, or other factors. If you don't make profound, lasting, system-wide changes, you can expect more and more turnover.

Maybe your company just sucks at allowing a work/life balance. More and more, the performance of your employees will suffer if there isn't a proper balance. You can mitigate this problem by offering a flexible schedule, paid time off, and fair expectations.

Remember this: *just because you are an overachiever doesn't mean your employees shouldn't have breaks or flexible schedule options.*

Though reasons for employee alienation and the resulting turnover vary, many are related directly to leadership. *Your* leadership. Consider the following problem areas:

1. **The employee's work purpose is unclear.**

   Most people want to feel like they are a part of something, and their work is important. If employees' goals aren't tied to organizational goals, how will they know their everyday work matters?

2. **Your communication with the employee is poor or sporadic.**

   In fact, studies show only half of the employees say their supervisor checks in with them regularly. To improve your communication, you'll want to consider which channels and platforms are most appropriate. Beyond that, you need to implement a multi-channel communication approach. Doing this means you understand your audience and know best how to meet their expectations and needs.

3. **There are inter-team conflicts you haven't handled effectively.**

   Honestly, people have conflicts all the time, and healthy conflict is actually a good thing. It helps with innovation, it encourages teams to hold themselves accountable, and it produces results. But when not handled well, conflict can turn bad and into petty arguments. Help your team learn how to deal with issues quickly and directly. Don't be the go-between. When it comes to dealing with problems, teach your employees to fish.

4. **You've not tuned in to employee burnout and stress.**

   Symptoms of burnout can include difficulty focusing, fatigue, overworking, low productivity, and overall malaise. Ways to counteract burnout are encouraging your employees to take breaks, blocking off time from work, and prioritizing employee physical and mental health. In addition, you can advocate for getting some sunshine exposure each day, catching up with friends, taking a daily walk, or volunteering. You can promote the idea of a dedicated and creative workspace for remote workers. If you really want to do the right thing, you'll pay for that remote space. And most importantly, give your employees some autonomy and control to avoid burnout--and find a way to celebrate small wins weekly.

## 5. You don't use agendas for meetings.

This might feel insignificant, but without a plan, you're flat-out wasting resources and time. However, with an agenda, you stay on track with meeting items, encourage employee participation, and ensure vital topics are covered. An agenda also means a late employee knows exactly where the meeting is when they enter the room, and speakers on the agenda know when they're up. Since meetings are necessary for every work environment, be the leader who does them smartly and efficiently. This is more likely to engage your employees.

## 6. You aren't handling remote management well.

A lot of managers were thrown off guard when their teams all had to work remotely. And many managers used it as an excuse not to lead their teams. No butts in seats made it impossible to see who the most dedicated worker was, who arrived first in the morning, who was the last to leave, and who ate at their desk and worked simultaneously through lunch. All these visual observations went away, so the bad managers who used these clues were stuck. Out of nowhere, managers had to actually lead their teams. Suddenly, they had to talk to people to find out what they were doing and put the processes in place to ensure the work was done. For some managers that was complex, and they didn't get the help they needed. Don't let that be you. If you don't know how to handle a remote team, ask for help.

# The Cost of Employee Turnover

To fully embrace the cost of employee turnover, let's take a look at a common scenario.

You have a fantastic software engineer, Tom, who earns $120k a year. Unfortunately, your *asshole* behavior caused Tom to leave. There's no going back, and it's going to cost you.

Let's walk through the actual costs of that turnover.

First, just by Tom walking out the door, the company is affected by the following losses:

| | |
|---|---|
| $200.00 | Administrative costs to cover his termination |
| $4,600.00 | Tom's accrued time off that you have to payout |
| $250.00 | Exit interview expenses |
| ------------- | |
| $5,050.00 | Total at this point |

Now, through an arduous search for a new software engineer, the following expenses have accumulated:

| | |
|---|---|
| $5,000.00 | Advertising |
| $2,000.00 | Cost of hiring manager's time to conduct interviews |
| $1,000.00 | Cost of recruiter's time to screen resumes |
| ------------- | |
| $13,050.00 | Total so far |

Your search led you to Jane. You've offered her the position, but you have to get her up to speed on the job:

| $20,000.00 | Lost productivity for the first six months |
|---|---|
| $5,000.00 | Training costs to the company |
| ------------- | |
| $38,050.00 | Total by now |

One last thing. When Tom left, a profitable account went with him. Factor in that loss:

| $10,000.00 | Loss of business opportunity |
|---|---|
| $1,000.00 | Project slippage, scope creep, and missed deadlines |
| ------------- | |
| $49,050.00 | GRAND TOTAL COST OF VERY BAD LEADERSHIP |

Like a snowball rolling downhill, replacing Tom has become increasingly costly. And keep in mind, these are conservative estimates. If it's a difficult role to fill or if your organization needs agency help, the costs could triple. Eventually, your company will notice what's going on, and soon, you won't be able to make enough excuses to cover your terrible behavior as a boss.

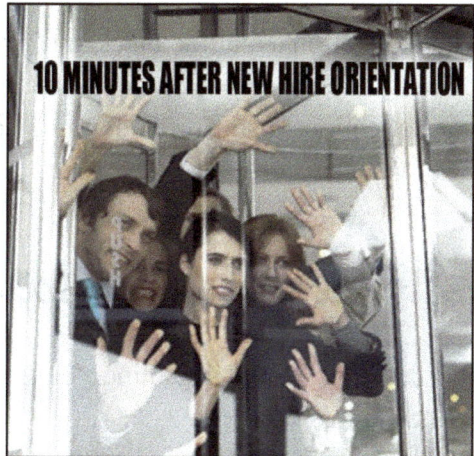

10 MINUTES AFTER NEW HIRE ORIENTATION

# Bringing It All Together

Employee turnover is no walk in the park. It's time-consuming and expensive to replace team members, so this chapter presents some reasons for turnover you might not have considered in an effort to be proactive.

Does your organization need to improve its training? Perhaps it doesn't provide growth opportunities. Or is your overall hiring process inefficient? Worse, is there perhaps a workplace culture issue? Seems like a lot, right?

If you thought it couldn't get any worse than those obstacles, consider this: *does your organization suck the life out of your employees, preventing a healthy work/life balance?*

*Ouch!*

I then shared how employees need their leader to provide purpose, frequent communication, effective conflict resolution, and tactics to avoid burnout and stress. I even pointed out something as minor as not having agendas for a meeting, which wastes everyone's time and is a significant problem

Finally, we looked at the black and white cost of replacing an employee. If nothing else gets a bad leader's attention, I hope this will. It's time to turn your attention to self-reflection and solutions for this very expensive and inconvenient problem.

# Self-Reflection & Solutions

It's that time again! Examine yourself by asking the following questions related to this chapter:

- *What responsibility do you have when it comes to controlling the turnover on your team?*
- *What are you doing to keep your turnover as low as possible?*
- *If you were to calculate the cost of turnover on your team, how comfortable would you be defending that expense to the CEO or Board of Directors?*
- *When you think about the last time you received feedback, what actions did you take for improvement based on what you were told?*
- *How comfortable are you not being the smartest person in the room?*

**TIP 1**

Conduct stay interviews.

Stay interviews can be really helpful to control turnover. Stay interviews are the opposite of exit interviews, and they aren't the same as an employee engagement survey. You want to talk to your high performers and find out the reasons they stay with the organization. Ask questions about their role, the company culture, and them as a person.

Some questions you could ask include the following:

- *What are the things that keep you here at our organization?*
- *Do you find meaning in purpose in your work? Why or why not.*
- *If you could change one thing about your job, what would you change and why?*
- *What do you like most/least about your job?*
- *What do you like most/least about the company?*
- *Which of your skills are you not using in your current role?*
- *Do you feel recognized for the work that you do?*

- *Have you been given the tools and resources to be successful at your job? If yes, what are they? If not, what's missing?*

You can also throw in my favorite questions, what should we *Start, Stop, and Continue* doing to create the best employee experience possible at our organization.

This stay interview should be a meeting, not an email. This is important information, and you want to make sure that you listen to the answers and, if possible, observe the body language. If you as a leader have not created a safe enough space for your team to feel comfortable giving you honest answers, yeah, *you're an asshole boss*, and now you have to find someone that they do trust to get these answers for you so you can make the right behavioral changes. Hopefully, there's a good person that can do this meeting for you, either in your leadership team or in HR.

---

**TIP 2**

Have an employee retreat.

---

While it would be great to take your employees on an all-expense-paid trip to the beach or the mountains, you don't have to do anything as extravagant as that to help your team move toward high performance. Taking your team out of their normal everyday work environment and focusing on something like goal planning, clarifying roles and responsibilities, updating your mission, vision, and values can help your team tremendously.

This doesn't have to be offsite, but it should definitely be someplace where your team can disconnect from their day-to-day responsibilities. I have seen some awesome company strategies come out of a two-day offsite retreat. Be creative, I once attended a meeting that was held at the zoo in a building attached to the back of the lion exhibit. Having a lion roar in seeming disagreement to what someone says is priceless!

Don't assume that just because you know how your team impacts the company goals that everyone on your team does. Don't take it for granted that your entire team is perfectly clear about what they should and shouldn't do in their roles. If you are seeing high turnover, almost certainly your team doesn't understand how what they do is connected to what other people in the company do. Take a day to help them understand the connections and what happens in the process before and after their involvement.

> **TIP**
> Reach out to former employees.

Some of your former employees may not do an exit interview on their way out. It could be that people are a little upset or tense when they give their resignation and prepare to leave the organization. Other people don't want to do an exit interview because they want to be truthful, but they may not be able to be *truthful* and *tactful* at that time.

With this realization, give it some time and then reach out. Ask the employee what caused them to leave the company.

A note of caution: you may not like what you hear, but it's very important information that you need to hear and let sink in.

Don't get upset, and definitely don't make excuses. If someone is willing to take time to talk to you once they've already left your organization, they're giving you the gift of their time and their feedback.

Make sure that they know that. Make sure you treat it as such. Most importantly, *do something* with that gift. Take action based on the feedback and incorporate what you learn into your leadership journey.

# YOUR EMPLOYEES KNOCK (OR DON'T KNOCK) ON YOUR DOOR

*Is your office door always closed? Are you approachable?*

The closed door might be hypothetical in this day and age, but think about it this way.

Have you asked yourself lately how often your employees come to you for follow-up, help, or just to say hello?

I know. You're a manager with many responsibilities. With so much on your to-do list, it's easy to get caught up in the day's busyness. Your head is usually down, and you're focused on whatever project is most pressing.

Your boat is so overloaded that you're ignoring emails, messages, and your team.

So, when someone from your team knocks on your door, literally or figuratively, you may be responding with a scowl without even realizing it. If you think this reaction makes employees feel safe in approaching you, you guessed right, *NO!*

Let's switch roles for a minute and consider this from a new employee's point of view.

Imagine starting a new job after being out of work for months. You've gone through your savings, and this job is keeping you and your family out of the homeless shelter. You're relieved and happy that you'll be able to keep up with your mortgage, feed your children, and have health insurance. Things were getting pretty stressful, but thankfully, you'll have a fresh start with this new company.

Needless to say, you have a lot riding on your success here.

You're upbeat, hopeful, and full of potential. However, you gradually notice during your first week that your boss isn't around much. You have a lot to do, though, so you don't think much about it. You're not worried.

But now, a few weeks have passed. In that time, you've had a grand total of 30 minutes of face-to-face time with your boss.

*30 whole minutes.*

Understandably, you're starting to feel a little lost. Your onboarding "buddy" has been great, but she doesn't know everything. Plus, she has her own projects going on, and you don't want to be a bother.

When you accepted the job, you decided against being a remote employee because the manager made it clear that *you being in the office* was her preference. You also hoped to spend as much time with her as possible to get a quick handle on your job and build work connections.

But it seems like that didn't really matter after all. It's a little confusing, to be honest.

When you're in your office, the manager's door is closed. You've learned enough during your brief time there to know when her door is closed, you shouldn't knock.

In fact, you experienced it firsthand your first week. You knocked on her door, and there was no answer.

So, you went back to your desk and thought she'd passed by while you weren't paying attention.

A few minutes later, she walked out of her office and right past you.

You looked over at your onboarding buddy, who laughed and said, "When she's *in the zone*, there's no disturbing her."

So, you asked, "What's the best way to get her attention?"

And your colleague shrugged before saying, "I don't know. I've been trying to figure it out for months."

This whole thing has left you feeling unsettled. I mean, you can't talk to your manager or learn from her if her door is always closed. Or if the manager has clearly communicated that she's too busy to guide you.

# Leadership Letdown

Now, when it's time for your 30-day check-in as a new employee, you mention the work that you couldn't complete because you needed the manager's input.

Your manager reacts with surprise. So, you try to explain what happened when you approached her for help.

She responds with something like, "My door is always open, so next time, try harder."

Besides being ignored, you've been reprimanded and dismissed.

Now you're completely freaked out because you have so much riding on this job.

And you can't help but notice that for someone whose door is supposedly "always open," there's *a whole lot* of unapproachable vibe going on.

Quite frankly, you're frustrated, too, because you can't get your job done on time without her input.

Wow. As an employee and not a manager, can you imagine what that feels like?

Employees are entirely dependent on their job for their livelihood, but it seems like sometimes they may not be successful because of the very person whose job it is to make sure they *are* successful.

As a manager, take a minute and let that soak in.

Truly, an employee could lose everything because of a manager's lack of self-awareness.

From the manager's perspective, they consider themselves available to their team, which isn't always true and can lead to a massive disconnect.

This kind of disconnect could cost someone their livelihood.

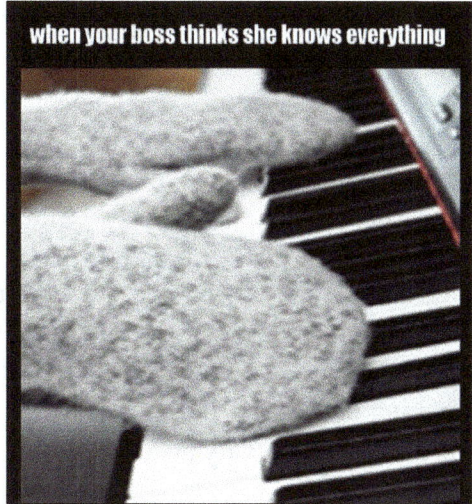

when your boss thinks she knows everything

Now think about yourself as a leader. Have you ever made anyone feel like this?

Unfortunately, I have.

I know what you might be thinking. *Why the heck should I listen to someone who did something so horrible?*

Here's the short answer. I learned from my mistake and didn't want anyone else to repeat it. So, let me explain.

## Regret and Remorse

Many, many years ago, I had a small staff, most of whom were responsible for payroll and HRIS work.

I'd been there for a few years, and we'd recently changed HRIS and payroll systems. Frankly, my team did an excellent job with the change.

So, when we got a new team member, I thought they would seamlessly fit in and work at the same speed as the other people on the team. After all, the system was new-ish for all of us.

I gave bare-bones training for the new employee and then busied myself, expecting the new hire to just figure things out.

I, of course, said to come to me with any questions they had.

I didn't even *have* a door at that time since we were in a little cube farm. Looking back at my body language and tone of voice, I realize that when the employee actually asked, I put up an entire wall—not just a door.

As you'd expect, the employee stopped asking, and they were significantly less than successful in the role.

The way I discovered my faux pas was embarrassing. I started a new job, and sure enough, my new boss ignored me hardcore.

I mean, they barely gave me the time of day. I remember sitting in my office one day with my door open. I was looking at my manager's closed door and thinking, *what an asshole!*

I mean, I couldn't imagine anyone would not make themselves available, at least for the first few weeks, to a new hire.

As I was admonishing them, I said to myself, ugh, who does that! Then a tiny voice in the back of my brain said, *"YOU!"*

*You did that!*

It's true. I was everything I'm telling you not to be.

*Dismissive.*

*Closed off.*

*Unavailable.*

In fact, I had higher expectations than I should have and didn't communicate them effectively. I didn't treat the team as individuals, I just expected someone new to jump in, and things would still run like a well-oiled machine.

And what was the consequence? The employee left the organization after a few months and had awful things to say about me.

I have to admit that most of those things were very true, though I brushed them off at the time.

My lack of self-awareness, experience, and concern for the new hire's learning style caused profound misery. I look back with such a massive amount of regret. After realizing my part in this terrible situation, it has been my secret shame for many years. Not being open to my employee, both figuratively and literally, had devastating effects.

I'm coming clean because I can't write a book about being a better leader by being authentic and vulnerable without doing those things myself.

If I could travel back in time to my early twenties and shake the *shit* out of myself, I would if it would stop me from hurting that employee. Then I would tell my younger self what I know now.

When you hire someone, you have a duty to make sure they have the best onboarding experience possible. As the manager, it was my job to ensure new hires were successful. I didn't do my job, and I blamed the attrition on the new employee. I took no ownership.

I would tell myself that I was *an asshole boss.*

# Closed Door = Closed Off

Closing your door means you won't know what's going on with your team, and your perspective will be skewed. Your employees will feel walled off from you, and an us-versus-them mentality could start to grow.

On the other hand, open doors lead to transparency.

An open door also encourages a culture of empowerment and equality, and it decreases favoritism in the workplace.

Let's consider a few more reasons to implement an open-door policy of your own, even if your company doesn't require it.

1. An open-door policy leads to collaboration and mutual trust.

   In earlier chapters, we've already established the importance of trust with employees, but I'll hammer it home again. Employees who trust and feel trusted have higher loyalty and achieve higher productivity. Collaboration will soar in a workplace with an accessible manager who can be trusted.

2. An open-door policy helps employees who have been victimized or harassed at work.

   Verbal or physical harassment interferes with employees' ability to work. The atmosphere becomes hostile, intimidating, or offensive. As management, you can create a safer environment with an open-door policy. Employees feel they can talk to you, and those harassing may be deterred because you're right there.

3. An open-door policy prevents confusion and rumors.

This type of behavior is incredibly toxic to workplaces. Allowing employees to openly approach you and communicate with you can proactively avoid unnecessary rumors and confusion.

4. An open-door policy welcomes effective communication between management and employees.

Enough said.

To be fair, there are some cons to an open-door policy. I'll just mention them here so you can be aware and on guard.

1. An open-door policy could create dependency.

When you're available to solve problems, some employees could become overly dependent on you. You want to guide them, but make sure they continue to grow and solve problems independently.

2. An open-door policy may disrupt the chain of command.

Some employees may go above your head to other higher-level executives, creating issues between them and the manager they should be working with--you! This shouldn't really bother you much. If you have a good relationship with your manager, their first words to that employee will be something like, "Well, what did (insert your name) say when you talked to them about this?" Learn this and live by this: employees can go talk to whomever they want. It's how the leaders react that causes the problem.

3. *An open-door policy might affect a manager's time and productivity.*

Leaders who are available to employees can become overwhelmed with people popping their heads into chat. Remind your employees that your open-door policy is a problem-solving method, not an excuse to socialize.

# Bringing It All Together

Chapter 7 focused on your availability to your employees. Is your office door open? Do you provide a welcoming atmosphere? Specifically, I presented an example of a new employee who couldn't seem to get access to their manager, the very person who should be mentoring and training them When that employee mentioned it to their manager, the manager made them feel as if it was all their fault. I asked you to put yourself in their shoes. How did having that experience feel for you?

This chapter also not-so-gently demonstrated how much power you have, as a leader, to completely change a person's livelihood and their ability to support themselves and their families. I shared an example from many years ago in my own career that still causes grief when I think about it. I hope my lack of self-awareness can provide an a-ha! moment for you and help avoid the same situation.

The bottom line is this: if your office door is closed, you'll miss out on vital clues about what's happening in your department. Reasons to keep your door open include increasing collaboration and trust, protecting employees from harassment or victimization, preventing confusion and rumors, and facilitating effective communication between management and employees.

On the other hand, I wanted you to be aware of the disadvantages that come from an open-door policy, so I briefly pointed out to watch for unhealthy dependencies forming, the disruption in the chain of command, and your time and your productivity being negatively affected.

With these words of caution in mind, let's examine your availability a bit closer through self-reflection and related solutions.

## Self-Reflection & Solutions

After hearing my experience, consider the following questions:

- *What do you do for new hires?*
- *Do you make yourself available?*
- *Do you set clear expectations? If you do, great!*
- *What do you do on a regular basis with your team?*
- *Are you putting up walls with your tone and body language?*

Now, I have a direct, somewhat painful question.

What did it feel like to put yourself in the shoes of someone who could lose everything because of their manager's inability to understand the full ramifications of their actions or lack thereof?

> **TIP**
>
> Stay true to your word.

If you say you have an open door, you have to have one. If you have an actual door, pay attention to how often it's open. If you are remote or in a cube farm like me, pay attention to how you react to people who are using your "open door." Are you getting people coming back with more questions, or do people tend to stay away? Keep track of it, especially if you have a new hire.

Actually, forget just offering an open-door policy. Take that door off the hinges! An open door removes barriers and promotes open communication.

By keeping your door open, you're inviting employees to casually chat when they walk by. This is your opportunity to ask about their weekend, families, or hobbies.

THE LOOK ON MY BOSS'S FACE

WHEN I USE THE OPEN DOOR POLICY

Then take the open-door policy to the next level and check in with people every once in a while, so your team knows you are, in fact, approachable.

**TIP 2**

Find different ways to ask for feedback and take action on it.

One of the best ways to know if you're doing things the right way is to *ask* if you are. Get feedback from your team. Ask them what their perceptions are. Find out what changes you need to make to your current onboarding process so they feel more supported.

Remember, there is a trick to getting this feedback from employees. You can't just go willy-nilly asking what they think of you. If you haven't created a psychologically safe environment, you'll get fake answers that won't help you.

Fake feedback might even make things worse for you because you'll think things are going well when they aren't.

One good way to get better feedback is to do a quick *Start, Stop, and Continue* exercise. If you haven't done it before, it's fairly simple.

You ask the person what you need to start doing to make things better, what you need to stop doing to make things better, and what things you can continue to do that are going well.

One out-of-the-box way of doing things is to reward constructive feedback. When someone tells you about something you did wrong or provides criticism, give them a small reward. Consider a $5 Starbucks gift card or free lunch, something simple to let them understand that you appreciate the gift of their feedback.

Or start by being critical of yourself. Say, *I recognize now I did a pretty lousy job of new hire training. What else have I dropped the ball on?*

Then actually *use* the feedback to *change* the behavior. And this is super important; when you do, let the people who gave you the feedback know that your change is thanks to the gift they gave you. If people know you're willing to make changes, they'll be more open to giving you more and more constructive feedback.

M
A
I
L

Be mindful.

Start paying attention to your surroundings. Be mindful of the time you spend with your head down, focused on getting things done yourself, when you should be leading your team.

One way to become more aware is a time study, which can help you remain mindful of when you are doing things for yourself and when you are doing things for your team.

This process doesn't have to be time-consuming and cumbersome. Keep a digital record or jot things down—it's totally up to you—but by taking a few minutes at the top of every hour to reflect on and writing down what you just spent the last hour doing, you access powerful and informative details about your time.

The first time I did a time study, I discovered that I spent about two full hours a day playing *Angry Birds*.

Embarrassing, to say the least. But it helped me pinpoint my own problems and where I was letting my team down.

It was a little like the airline thing. I had to put on my own mask before putting the mask on those people I was responsible for. That is, I had to solve my own problems and take care of myself before I could even begin to take care of someone else's problems.

Now it's time to figure out what's bogging you down and what you need to do to change your leadership behavior.

# HR IS CONSTANTLY ON YOUR BACK

### Are there multiple complaints about you and your management style?

How many times have your employees gone to Human Resources for help to deal with you? *Spoiler alert:* the answer should be close to zero. Every once in a while, you may have an honest misunderstanding with an employee. That happens to the best of people.

However, if you find yourself in the HR office time and time again, dealing with complaint after complaint, the problem is probably *you*. The good news is if you have a competent HR team, they will immediately understand what the problem is and get you the help you need to be a better leader.

The major problems happen when the HR team isn't so great, and they don't immediately recognize you are the problem.

Let's chat about what was, hands down, my worst experience with a leader to date.

## Meet Brian

Several years ago, I supported a leader who was not from the US. We're going to call him Brian. I knew I was in for some trouble when, in my first week supporting him, as his HR professional he told me he didn't give a hoot about our silly American laws because we are softies over here.

Brian was petty, mean, and insanely rude. He talked down to everyone, talked trash about everyone, and could spend hours talking about how great he was. He was so great, in fact, an indigenous tribe made him an honorary king. Yeah.

He thought that highly of himself. He was absolutely awful. Brian purposefully intimidated people. He would change his mind about something last minute and berate people for not keeping up with what was going on in his mind. He was the definition of a dumpster fire, and a lot of people complained about him. I coached, counseled, and cajoled.

Nothing worked.

Otherwise, the company I worked for was a delight. They paid really well, the staff was down-to-earth and friendly, and I loved going to work every day. Incredibly tight-knit, the people I worked with every day were intelligent and caring. We were really like a little family. The department was like a puzzle, and we all perfectly fit. It was inclusive, and for me, at least, I felt like I belonged.

It wasn't utopia, of course. We disagreed and got snippy with each other, but at the end of the day, we were a team working towards the organization's goals. Brian was the only fly in the ointment.

So, with all Brian's undesirable traits mentioned above, the final straw was when he put the brakes on a job offer going out to someone for one of his open roles. Brian's reason? They were transgender, and he felt like hiring her would make him a laughingstock. He said the workplace wasn't ready for it, and he wasn't going allow himself to be the target of mockery.

Big no-no, right?

It was wildly inappropriate and, of course, mean-spirited, but it was totally legal at that time.

In an effort to make Brian see reason, I asked him to consider if it was my father coming to him for a job. I asked him to imagine if this happened when it was legal to turn down Black people based solely on the color of their skin.

With that scenario, I asked Brian, would he turn my father away even if it *was* legal?

I expected Brian to shift his mindset after looking at it through that lens. What I didn't expect was his answer. *No, he said, he would not.*

He would not hire my father.

I felt like a horse had kicked me.

So now I'm faced with this awful situation. This leader wanted to do something morally wrong and also admitted he was okay with racism.

All I could do was sit there with my mouth open. Not my finest moment.

I've said it before in this book; I have my flaws. I have bias. I know that.

And one of them is that when someone has an accent, I automatically assume they are intelligent, refined, and cultured. I realize this is ridiculously stupid, and I can't pinpoint when in my childhood this thought wormed its way into my head. But the point here is this awful leader had a killer accent, so the dichotomy was tearing my brain apart.

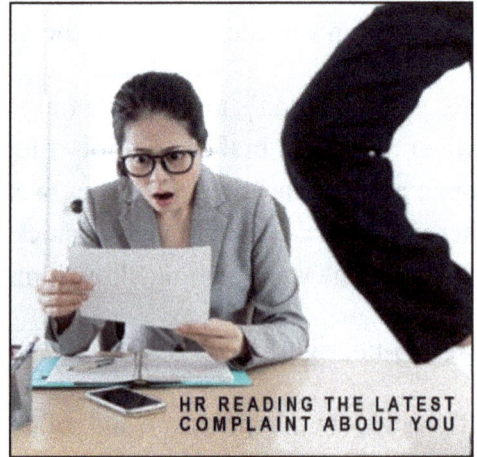

HR READING THE LATEST COMPLAINT ABOUT YOU

When the two halves of my brain finally came back together, I called my leader, who told me I was correct: we should move forward with the hire. She would run this up the flagpole, and Brian was finally going to be held accountable for his bad behavior.

Only, that's not what happened.

Instead, I was transferred.

Brian didn't hire the woman.

And I lost faith in my leader, her leader, and the organization as a whole.

# Damaged and Distraught

I won't lie, that experience was almost the end of my HR career. To this day, when I really think about it and put myself back in that situation, I'm near tears.

I failed that applicant. I hope she went on to find a role and an organization that valued her because she was an incredible candidate, and we would have been lucky to have her.

But my company failed me.

So, I left.

I stayed in touch with a few people from the company and heard when Brian's horrible behavior eventually bit them in the ass. Brian's inability to see people as human beings led him to say something rude to a person who the company valued more than him. So eventually, Brian got booted.

But that didn't happen for nearly a full year after I left the company. For me, it didn't resolve anything. It didn't bring solace.

And it sure didn't change the *shitty* management and HR practices that allowed Brian to do awful, horrible, bad things. Contrary to everything I believed to be true, HR let me down.

Before that situation, and sometimes even now, it boggles my mind when I read articles or hear people talking about the harmful ways their manager has treated them and the even more terrible responses of the HR team.

For example, one of the big buzzes going on right now is the Activision Blizzard lawsuit. This is a damaging case that'll probably end up in HR and law textbooks. The gist of it is that the company, which makes video games, had managers who misbehaved so badly that a woman died by suicide. Her death came after her boss, who she was in a relationship with, shared inappropriate pictures of her with coworkers.

The lawsuit alleges the Human Resources department was well aware of the many years of harassment and inappropriate behavior, but it did nothing to fix the problem.

As evidence, women were not given promotions because they may become pregnant. Women were given a hard time when they had to pick up their kids from daycare. And the rooms the company set aside for lactation were often used for meetings. Yep, they just kicked the lactating women out.

If you haven't heard about this case and your jaw dropped to your knees like mine did, that's a good thing.

Behavior like this should be shocking because it should *never, ever* happen. And the fact it did for years is appalling.

That HR team should be ashamed of themselves. But the blame doesn't lie entirely on them. There was an entire leadership team that was aware of the ongoing issues. So, it didn't matter if an employee filed a complaint, and the manager was investigated by HR. There were no repercussions.

Whether you call it the *People Team*, *Human Capital*, *Human Resources*, or use another title, the overall goal should always be to ensure employees have the best employee experience possible.

It's *not* about protecting leaders.

It's *not* about keeping the company out of litigation.

It *is* about doing the right thing every single time.

After all, there's no need to be a compliance cop if you're doing the right thing. The company won't have to worry about litigation if they are doing the right things.

Accordingly, the HR department shouldn't be punitive. *It should add value.* It should be a department everyone can count on for help, growth, and development.

With this in mind, leaders in every organization must understand their duty to do the right thing. Employees aren't there as playthings and toys. They are human beings, depending on their leaders for everything. I mean everything. Messing with someone's employment is messing with their entire lives.

This becomes a major problem with an *asshole boss*, because having someone being so reliant on them brings out terrible behavior, especially in people who are crave power. It's unfortunate but sometimes the wrong people are promoted into management roles, creating situations where someone who has no business having the livelihood of others at their disposal being the person who can make decisions to hire, fire, promote, or even end someone's career.

In fact, those managers are why companies need strong HR teams and strong executive teams who *listen* to HR.

Bottom line. If you, as a manager *work somewhere with a strong HR team* and *you're fielding complaint after complaint about your behavior* then it's time to stop and take a hard look at what you're doing and how it impacts the people around you.

# Bringing It All Together

This chapter took an honest and somewhat uncomfortable look at what to do when HR is constantly approaching you about employee complaints. A genuine misunderstanding with an employee is reasonable from time to time, but I'm talking about HR having to field complaint after complaint about you.

I introduced you to Brian, the arrogant, intimidating, and rude bully who turned out to possess the bonus traits of disgusting racism. After I'd had enough of Brian's blatant conduct, I talked to my supervisor, who agreed that Brian was out of line and wouldn't get away with it any longer.

Except that was all hogwash. I was transferred, and Brian kept doing his dirty deeds. Even though Brian dug his own grave and was finally brought down a year later, I have to admit, HR had failed me.

As a leader, don't be a Brian. You should do the right thing at the right time all the time and every time! And HR should be there to help you along the way.

Remember, if you're being complained about frequently, it's time to take responsibility and figure out how to improve.

# Self-Reflection & Solutions

We've arrived once again at that time. Take a look at your behavior by asking questions related to this chapter:

- *How well-versed are you in what is and is not acceptable (or legal or illegal) to say to your employees?*
- *Check in with your moral compass. When was the last time you veered off track and realized your compass wasn't pointing true north? What was that situation like, and how did you feel when it happened?*
- *How would you answer if someone asked you to do something you knew was immoral or wrong?*

- *Have you ever asked someone on your team to do something they may not have been comfortable with? What happened in that situation, and what, if anything, would you change if you had a do-over?*
- *When someone does complain about you, what is your reaction? Is it productive, or does it continue to exacerbate the problem?*

> **TIP 1**
>
> Get a 360 Leadership Assesment.

We introduced this in Chapter 1 as a way to understand why your employees might stop talking when you enter a room. As you can imagine, though, this assessment reveals powerful information in multiple areas. If you're having trouble with HR, I can't stress enough how vital this step can be. Let's learn more.

A good 360 Leadership Assessment looks at competencies such as:

- your strengths
- your areas needing improvement
- your composure under pressure
- your listening skills
- your communication aptitude
- your problem-solving skills
- your capacity to lead
- your ability to include others
- your competence to plan and set goals
- your receptiveness to input and feedback
- your ability to self-regulate
- your talent in providing beneficial input to your team

- your ability to motivate others

Don't let this list overwhelm you! No one has strengths in all areas. In fact, no one expects you to be strong in all areas and every aspect. But by understanding your skill level in each area, your management flourishes.

The following are the benefits of investigating your leadership abilities through a 360 Leadership Assessment:

- You receive honest feedback (not just what employees think you want to hear).
- One-sided feedback is eliminated.
- You'll gain trust and respect.
- Your self-awareness grows.
- Meaningful conversations are encouraged.
- Your company's spirit and culture will improve.

Remember, feedback can be your friend because *you can't fix what you don't know about*. Leaders aren't usually aware of their *blind spots* (hence the term blind spots).

Keep in mind, too, that a 360 Leadership Assessment is a reflection of others' perceptions of you. It doesn't mean it's a complete or valid picture of who you are as a person.

It analyzes you in a *specific* role at a *particular* moment in time in a *certain* context and culture.

That said, you can more easily change someone's perception of you than change who you are. A 360 Leadership Assessment gives you data to help you improve, which will help change the perceptions of those around you.

Before we move on, here are a few pro tips about interpreting your assessment results:

1. **Focus on what you do well rather than your weaknesses.**

   It's a sign of resilience to focus on building your strengths.

2. **Write down positive feedback.**

   These kudos are given confidentially and freely, so savor them. Use them for inspiration on challenging days.

3. **Determine two or three areas of weakness to work on.**

   Consider what areas of weakness surprised you. How can you address those for a few quick wins?

After the 360 Leadership Assessment results are in, you must take the time to thank your raters. Share what you learned and what you're working on. Then ask for their ongoing feedback and support.

In the end, the 360 Leadership Assessment is meant to provide a clear plan for moving forward. You'll need to integrate your goals into your daily routine to stay focused.

---

**TIP 22**

Get a mentor.

---

It may be time for you to develop a close relationship with someone who can help keep you out of trouble. If your company doesn't have a formal mentoring program, that's okay. Is there someone who has a strong team that you look at and wonder how they do it? Can you identify someone who doesn't look like you, act like you, or have a background similar to your own who's reasonably successful in the organization? Can your leader make a recommendation of someone who they think would be great to help you on your leadership journey?

You may find you want to find a mentor outside of your organization. If your organization is small and you can't identify anyone who would be beneficial, this may be the case. But if you're looking externally because you are embarrassed or anything along those lines, I urge you to work through it and go the first route. Having a mentor who understands the inner workings of the company where you both work is invaluable. Many companies provide mentoring services to professionals, some even at no cost.

A mentor is different than a coach, and if you are truly struggling as a leader, coaching may not be the right solution for you in the beginning. Coaching is a slower process that tends to have longer-lasting results, but if your situation is dire, you may need a quick boost to help you more immediately correct undesirable behavior.

It may be that getting a mentor and hearing the perspective of someone outside of your usual group is enough of an eye-opening experience that your behavior changes, and you never have a complaint again. But don't expect overnight success. Good things never come easy. Becoming a great leader is a challenging process with ups and downs. You just need to ride it out and know in the end, you will be a better person for having taken that journey.

I'll admit that I'm a bit biased when it comes to what your HR team should and shouldn't do. In my opinion, (*hey, you bought the book*) one of the best things you can do to understand the problems is to go to the person receiving the complaints and ask them for help.

Whoever is supporting you from an HR standpoint should be able to help you learn more about what you are doing wrong and what you can do to get better.

| | |
|---|---|
| **T I P** | Ask HR for help. |

Leadership development is one of the most important things that a Human Resources department can do to help an organization be successful. They should be staffed so that you can go to them for help without fear of repercussions or retaliation.

# IT'S YOUR WAY OR THE HIGHWAY

*You're the leader, so you make all of the decisions. Shouldn't employees just follow you without question?*

You're running a brainstorming session, and everyone seems pretty jazzed to be there.

Participation is high, you're getting input from most people on the team, and it seems like everyone is engaged and having a good time. People are discussing their ideas, and there is a lot of chatter in the room. So far, it's all smiles, and it seems like most people on the team have had something to say and contribute to the conversation. You're happy that everyone is participating, but you aren't happy with what they are actually saying.

As the meeting goes on, you don't agree with most of their ideas, so you don't capture them, but you appreciate the effort everyone is putting in. They just aren't providing options that line up with *your* vision.

After ten minutes or so, you notice the vibe has shifted. People are sitting back in their chairs with their arms folded across their chests. Others are checking their phones or just sitting there with frowns on.

But you continue. And you give opinion after opinion. Idea after idea.

What happened to that enthusiastic vibe? Did your brainstorming session turn into a validation session? Or even worse, do you walk into brainstorming sessions and immediately put your idea out there and ask for feedback? Do you think someone is going to speak up and tell you what a horrible idea you have, particularly in the painfully awful culture you've created on your team?

Sounds a lot like someone who says they are open to feedback, but they really aren't. This manager's actions don't match their words at all. They might be good at soliciting feedback, but they don't actually care about the feedback, and ideas that don't support their exact vision are completely disregarded.

## Meet Greg

I used to work with a leader named Greg, who would say that if he ever got in the way of things going well, he would step away immediately and let someone else run the show. He must've said this a dozen times during the first few months of me working there. He assured me he wanted someone who would be honest, advise him on what was working, and point out what wasn't working.

Turns out that couldn't have been further from the truth.

When Greg got in the way, he stubbornly dug in his heels instead of moving to the sidelines. In a flagrant display of a lack of self-awareness, he disregarded the feedback provided in a 360 Leadership, stating it didn't give a complete picture.

Needless to say, this trend continued. Greg would ask for input and then disregard it completely. As most people could guess, this wasn't received very well by his employees. But somehow, he missed that. It never even crossed his mind there was anything wrong with this.

Things just got worse and worse.

Greg would redo work employees had already done, causing confusion and miscommunication.

He would ask multiple people to do the same task, forget who he asked, then get mad at the wrong person for not doing it.

He played favorites and lived by a *what have you done for me lately* mentality.

If an employee did something wrong, all hell would break loose, even if that same employee saved the day last week.

Another awesome thing that started happening was around the clock working.

Ok, ok, I realize I'm probably the last person to speak up against 24-hour days.

*Pot, meet kettle.*

But I work a lot because I love what I do, and I pay myself. When I'm leading a team, I make sure I lead by example and don't send emails at 1 am. And I certainly wouldn't expect someone to answer immediately if I did.

Good ol' Greg. He didn't believe in work/life balance. It seemed like he didn't believe in anything but work.

Sure, working around the clock to meet a deadline is something that happens.

But working around the clock all the time is something that should *never* happen. It should *never* be an expectation, and people should *never* be penalized for not wanting to.

what they mean when they say needs to work well under pressure

But when Greg wanted something done, it was his way or get the hell out of the company.

Work sunup to sundown. Holidays didn't exist. Vacations were canceled. He did a lot of bad things.

And boy, if he got a dime for every piece of feedback *Greg the Great* rejected, he could have fed a family of five for a year. But from the beginning, he insisted he was open to feedback and innovative ideas, claiming to be dripping in self-awareness.

The end of the story? You guessed it. Greg's team not only hated him, but he had a hard time recruiting new team members, the company's reputation tanked, and they struggled to keep people from resigning.

Things weren't getting done on time, and instead of looking at how what he was doing caused that, he pointed the finger everywhere else. He truly believed that the productivity problems came from people not following his every instruction.

You've must have guessed by now that Greg was the root of the problem. I don't know if he truly didn't care about the people on his team or just didn't know what he was doing, but either way, it manifested in horrible ways that caused many people a lot of trepidation.

Listen. Even if people mean nothing to you, you waste company time and resources when you exhibit lousy leadership behavior. There is an actual cost as a consequence of those actions. While I wish leaders did the right thing for the right reasons, if the bottom line is your only driver, I'm okay as long as you treat people well.

# Bringing It All Together

In our next-to-last chapter, we asked the question: is it really your way or the highway? And if it is, *should it be?*

I think we both know the answer to that.

I begged you in this chapter to *not* solicit feedback and then totally disregard it for your own agenda. A huge part of maturity is being able to accept feedback and implement it to improve your team.

And when things go wrong, as they so often can, avoid finger-pointing and accept that you may have caused the problem. Like Greg, you can't keep doing your own thing at the expense of your employees forever.

You must examine your actions and words—do they match? The next section will help you decide and then take action for lasting change.

After all, there's enough room on the highway for all of us.

# Self-Reflection & Solutions

It's that time again where you look back at your behavior and ask the questions addressed in this chapter:

- *What drives the need for you to be the first person to give an opinion?*
- *How would your behavior change if you view your employees as finite resources rather than replaceable?*
- *What might happen if you're wrong or make a mistake and openly admit that to your team?*
- *Have you properly assessed the skills of everyone on your team so you know who can give the best ideas or solutions, depending on what the problem is?*
- *What happened the last time you listened to someone's ideas?*

| | |
|---|---|
| **TIP** | Brainstorm effectively. |

The whole point of brainstorming is to get the ideas of others because you realize your answer may not be the only correct approach or the best way to get something done.

When you brainstorm, you should get a bunch of other ideas and solutions for whatever the problem is. Sometimes the most farfetched, crazy, this-will-never-work idea actually works! If you walk into a brainstorming session knowing you already have the answer, just turn around and walk back out again. It will be evident to everyone in there that you don't want or value their opinions.

Instead, start the brainstorming session with a clear head, focused on the issue. Let people know that *no idea is a bad idea*. You may even want to give someone a prize at the end for the craziest idea.

And don't start the session by giving your opinion. In fact, you may want to wait until the very end to let people know your thoughts to avoid impacting what the team shares. Avoid being snarky, belittling people, or any other type of bad leadership behavior. That will shut down the conversation immediately, and then you're just left with your idea, which honestly might not be as great as you think it is.

> ### CLUE 29
>
> use different approaches to problem solving.

Depending on the problem, I love doing a *Start, Stop, Continue* exercise to start brainstorming sessions. It is easy to do, and you can learn a lot in a very short amount of time.

The exercise is done exactly as it sounds.

153

1. Start.

   Think about the subject. Then ask questions like: *What needs to be done to improve this situation? What would make it better, more effective, or less costly?* Personalize this to your circumstances.

2. Stop.

   What do you need to stop doing? What isn't working?

3. Continue.

   What *is* working? What should you continue doing?

This exercise is a great way to focus the conversation, keep it positive, and make sure that you walk away with clear action items.

Sometimes, you may go back and forth between the items based on what comes up in the conversation. For instance, you may get to the first step and realize that, in order to start, you need to stop something else. That's OK. In fact, that's great. It means you're no longer just scraping the surface.

You are really digging in and getting to actionable items that will help you resolve the issues you're working on.

If you are taking over a new team, this exercise can help you rapidly learn what's going well with your new team and what you may want to tackle first to make your team better.

You can also use *Start, Stop, Continue* with just about anything you are trying to improve, including a product, a process, or even a person.

I always liked doing this exercise when I had a new group to support as an HR professional. You get a unique perspective about the leader's understanding of HR's value, and you realize what can be done to either increase their expectations or exceed the ones they already have.

Let's say you have someone on your team who isn't performing well. This is a great way to help that person get back on track and discover if that person has the competency and skills to do the job. Or maybe you'll realize that you need to help that person find a role or an organization that would better suit their skills.

Either way, it can be a really powerful conversation that helps the employee determine their best course of action. You're able to give the employee a clear idea of the expectations of the role. Tell them what success looks like. Be detailed and abundantly clear.

Then ask the employee what they think that they should *start* doing to meet the expectations of the role, what they should *continue* doing, and what they should *stop* doing. If you are both being honest, this conversation should be enough to turn around just about any performance issues. At the end of the conversation, make some agreements and commitments to do the actions identified along with a timeline for completing them.

> **TIP**
>
> Listen effectively.

Sometimes, what you think you're hearing isn't what's actually being said.

With this realization, practice your active listening skills and focus on what is being said rather than what your response should be.

It's a really bad practice to shoot down an idea if you haven't *really* heard what was being said.

Remember to ask for clarification, ask questions, and summarize what you've heard so that you are sure that you have a clear understanding of what the person is trying to say. That sounds a bit like, *what I heard you say was that you feel like you not only don't have the tools and resources to perform your job well, but you also have no idea where to turn to for help. Did I hear what you are saying correctly?*

It's important to remember that even as the CEO, you not only can make mistakes, you absolutely will. We talked earlier about psychological safety and the importance of instilling this in your culture. Well, when no one has a say but you, how safe do you think your employees feel bringing anything up? Unless you want to be the next company pulling products from shelves or feeling the wrath of Twitter, start paying attention what those around you have to say. They may end up saving you from yourself.

# EVERYONE IS PROMOTED AT WORK BUT YOU

You feel like you're outpaced by everyone. Sure, you lead a team, but as far as career progression goes, you remain stagnant. Does it seem like everyone else is moving up except you?

You've been a leader of people for years. You feel like you know what you're doing, and you always get results. You've been the lead on several projects, and they have always been completed on time and under budget. You receive feedback from your manager that you're doing well in your position year after year. But that's just it; you've been in your position for years. It feels like forever.

You want to move up the ladder and into the C-Suite, but it hasn't happened yet, and it feels like it never will. Let's take a closer look at one such situation.

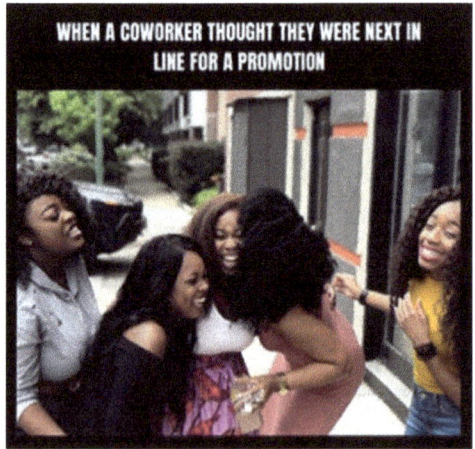

WHEN A COWORKER THOUGHT THEY WERE NEXT IN LINE FOR A PROMOTION

## Meet Hannah

Over a few years in one particular HR role, I supported Hannah as a leader. Simply put, Hannah was brilliant. She knew the job well, she got along beautifully with people, and she seemed to really motivate her team, who always rallied around her and consistently had great things to say about her.

Consequently, I was really baffled when I found out Hannah was passed over time and time again for a promotion. I couldn't for the life of me understand *why*, so me being me, I did some digging.

I discovered that her team was loyal to her. Very loyal but for all the wrong reasons.

You see, leaders need to be the buffer between their team and any negativity from upper leadership. They should be the ones to translate messages so that they aren't just palatable but invigorating.

Often, when a leader has a supervisor they don't get along with, those tensions are visible to the rest of the team. It's up to the leader to change that narrative and not let their relationship with their boss impact any other relationships on the team.

158

And that's where Hannah went wrong. She felt that her manager didn't like her. The two had some negative interactions over the years, which created a strained relationship between them. Unfortunately, Hannah let that strained relationship trickle down to her team, and her team let it trickle down to their teams.

Through some inquiry, I was able to find out that Hannah talked a lot of trash about her leader to her team. She convinced her team that her boss had it out for her and that they needed to make sure to get their work done on time and under budget, or they would all be fired. As a result, her team was getting stuff done but at what cost?

Getting things done isn't always the only thing that matters. *How* you get things done matters quite a bit more, especially when you get results by manipulation and gossip.

Hannah made her problem with her boss a problem for everyone in her department. And unfortunately, her manager knew about it. That meant when positions became available, Hannah wasn't considered for promotion because she made a very basic but damaging leadership mistake. *How you get your team motivated and engaged matters immensely.*

Hannah's supervisor knew that the higher up Hannah went, the worst her leadership style would be for the company. So instead of getting promoted, Hannah was barely holding on to her job because she discredited any feedback her manager gave her and made everything very personal. Hannah got away with her bad behavior for two reasons: 1. her team was getting stuff done, and 2. her manager was okay with taking one for the team. But the consequences were that Hannah certainly wasn't going to be promoted any time soon.

In fact, Hannah's manager had tried repeatedly. She gave Hannah consistent feedback throughout the years, but through Hannah's lens, the feedback was just another complaint from a manager that had it out for her from day one.

Truly, there was a lot that Hannah could've benefited from. Much of the feedback was directly related to her leadership style. She would do things like give an employee an extra day off without tracking it or allow remote work without clearing it through the proper channels.

While these seemed like tiny issues to Hannah, her manager understood that the higher up the organizational chart you go, the faster those minor issues become major problems.

And it doesn't look good when a senior leader's actions are contrary to the policies and procedures of the company. It looks even worse when it seems like a senior leader plays favorites by giving some people extra perks and not others.

The way Hannah curried favor put the company and her employees in a precarious position. Hannah acted as an agent of the company while at the same time doing things that went against company policy. She singlehandedly created a department that worked outside of the environment that the senior leadership team wanted to create.

So yes, Hannah's employees loved her but just her. They didn't love the company or the rest of the leadership team, so her actions didn't just jeopardize her own upward momentum. They hampered her entire team.

Let this be a powerful motivator for you. Even if your manager is the biggest *asshole* in the book, don't fall into the trap of helping *shit* roll downhill. It will do that enough on its own.

Instead, be the barrier and buffer that your team needs. Then, separately work on your relationship with your manager—and without involving anyone on your team. You are there to lead them, not to poison the well.

# Meet Andrew

Another leader I worked with also had a department that got things done well. But unlike Hannah, Andrew didn't have to tell his team bad things about his leader to gain their loyalty. What he did instead was not hold the people on his team accountable.

When Andrew's people didn't get work done, he did it himself.

If something was going to be late, he took care of it.

If they did something wrong, he corrected it. Then he covered it up by doing the work for them so that it would be done on time, and he wouldn't have to report any slippage in the schedule. He didn't hold them accountable in the least.

Andrew couldn't take on more responsibility because he was too busy doing the work of his entire team. For him, a promotion was out of the question.

Andrew had a team full of people happy to come to work every day. But they were just as unpromotable as him because they didn't have the competencies required to do their jobs well.

Andrew thought he was helping his team out by being flexible and kind, but in reality, he was sealing all of their fates by not leading them effectively.

# Bringing It All Together

In our last chapter, we asked a probing question: *Why is everyone else moving up but you aren't?*

To demonstrate, we met Hannah, who was brilliant and well-liked by her team. But Hannah turned her team into a little army that backed her no matter what, even if it meant alienating Hannah's supervisor. As a result, her team worked hard for her and produced quality work, but Hannah's supervisor knew what was happening and wouldn't let Hannah move up and further poison the organization.

I also introduced Andrew, who covered for his employees and didn't hold them accountable. His lack of leadership was a thorn in his side and kept him from moving up in the company.

Don't be like Hannah or Andrew. Don't let bad leadership behavior stop you from moving up the career ladder. Instead, take charge, identify your weaknesses, and make changes to ensure a fulfilling and lucrative career. You can begin by working through the next section for self-reflection and correction.

# Self-Reflection & Solutions

- *Think about the last time you got feedback from your leader. What was it, and how did you react to it?*
- *Reflect on your relationship with your team. Are you currying favor, or are you coaching and leading?*
- *What are your peers doing differently?*
- *If you truly believe that you have no ownership in your career growth, what can you do to develop agency?*

- *Are you practicing what you preach? Do you do the things that you tell your team to do when it comes to career development?*

Have an open and honest conversation with your leader about your performance. If you've done this before, make sure that you frame the conversation so that they know that this is a clean slate—be clear that you are willing to listen and learn this time around.

> **TIP 1**
>
> Be very direct.

Ask what you are doing well and what you need to work on to be promoted. If you disagree with their assessment, have a conversation about why you feel that way, but be open to being completely wrong.

I used to work for a company where one error could follow an employee for years.

I'm not joking. I remember having conversations with people about why they didn't want someone on their team, and their reasons would be about something that person did 10 or 20 years ago.

> **TIP 2**
>
> Give the organization a fair assessment.

People who want to grow and develop do so *over time*, and when someone holds a 10-year-old mistake against them, that isn't the right thing to do.

If you are truly doing all the right things, but your organization can't see your growth, it might be time to do a full assessment of the organization to determine if you are truly in the right place. Think about the conversations you've had with your leaders over the years. If they are not acknowledging your growth or giving you the tools you need to grow, it may be time for you to move on.

TIP 3

Take a good, long look in the mirror.

Have an honest conversation with yourself.

Have you really listened to feedback that you've been provided? Really think about it.

Go through the feedback in your mind, and then link that feedback to actions that you took to make changes. If you haven't taken any action, perhaps you are being an *asshole*, and you're getting in your own way.

# MOVE OVER A**HOLES; THERE'S A NEW LEADER IN TOWN

First, if you made it this far, thank you for sticking with me. I recognize that the world is a busy place, and your time is precious. I appreciate you taking time out of your busy life to read this book.

I don't have any complex methodology or framework. I just have one simple philosophy I hope all leaders begin to follow: *give employees the best experience possible*. If you lead with that at the forefront of your mind and actions, it will be very hard for you to go wrong.

At the time of this writing, we've suffered a global pandemic, there's a housing crisis, and record-high unemployment rates were followed by record-high job openings.

The traditional 40-hour workweek and hourly pay system aren't working anymore. Neither is the biased and sometimes discriminatory practices currently running rampant in many organizations.

Candidates are tired of being ghosted after taking time off to go to multiple interviews over the course of several weeks. They don't want to apply for hundreds of jobs and not hear back from anyone for months.

Retail employees don't want to be yelled at by customers only to have their manager take the customer's side, no matter what. Newsflash, the customer isn't always right. Waitstaff doesn't want to have to deal with sexual harassment from customers to get good tips. No one should have to put aside their dignity to get through the day when they go to work. No one should have to deal with being treated poorly so that they can have a roof over their heads and food in their bellies.

We are at a crossroads.

To put it bluntly, people are no longer dealing with *asshole bosses*. Many would rather do freelance or gig work, trading being their own boss for a higher rate of pay. What worked in the past to attract and retain employees just doesn't work anymore.

People demand flexibility, equity, and respect.

It shouldn't be hard to give people those things, yet some organizations are still struggling. Giving employees the best experience possible means that people need to take precedence over profits.

When companies focus on people first, they seem to thrive.

For example, Gravity Payments has a minimum wage as a company and pays their employees more than twice the amount of minimum wage they're legally required to pay. In another instance, Costco is famous for paying people a living wage.

Both of these are profitable companies that get publicity for doing good things rather than having their employees screaming horrible things about them from the rooftops.

You see, when companies do the right thing, not just for the accolades but for the right reasons, the rewards are not just monetary. Employees are happier, and as a leader, you will be happier as well.

So, what does this new leader look like?

Does it look about you?

The successful leader of the future is collaborative, innovative, strategic, authentic, accountable, inclusive, self-aware, open-minded, flexible, empathetic, and humble.

I worked for someone once who was, hands down, the best leader I ever had, and they had all of those skills. Because I had this leader very early on in my career, everyone else had big shoes to fill, and no one ever did. I am truly thankful that I had the opportunity to work for someone who was truly well before their time when it came to their leadership philosophy. However, I started off absolutely hating her.

Ok, as you read this, keep *reminding* yourself that I was very young when this happened.

Here we go.

A zillion years ago, the person I was working for was terminated, and their boss, Cindy, told me who was going to take their place. We'll call her Jess. I didn't have much of a relationship with Jess and was looking forward to learning more about her. But Cindy put a stop to that curiosity quickly. She let me know that Jess hated me, hated my department, and wanted to have me fired so that she could replace me with someone she liked better.

I was shocked.

I didn't know Jess and wasn't sure how she had come to that conclusion about me. I thought for sure that Cindy was wrong, but she assured me that she was not. When I asked Cindy if I could talk to Jess about it, she let me know that she would help me work through the relationship and that I shouldn't confront Jess about it because that would just make things worse.

I was floored. I wanted to go talk to Jess, but Cindy was a larger-than-life senior leader who flew into our site from the corporate office every couple of weeks that had significantly more experience than me at the time. And Cindy had such a dynamic personality. She was friendly and eccentric and absolutely beautiful. She was the kind of person that exuded confidence, and when she entered a room, everyone expected her to take over and lead whatever had been going on before she got there. She may as well have always walked around with a shirt that said, "I'm here. You can start now." Because of that, I trusted her judgment and went with her advice.

For the next several weeks, Jess and I butted heads. She would go to her office, walking right past mine without bothering to say *"Good morning."* We had only had one "official" meeting, and it was chilly and formal. I began to really dislike Jess because she had judged me so harshly and had so many negative thoughts about me for absolutely no reason. I'd done nothing to her.

Cindy continued to fly in and out, meeting with my team and relaying information she got from Jess and acting as a go-between. It was hard for me because I really enjoyed my job, my team was great, and there was so much room for my career growth. But according to Cindy, with a leader who hated me, I wasn't going to grow. I was going to GO.

When Cindy did her third or fourth visit, she eagerly let me know that I might have a much better time at work in the near future if I could just hold on for a while. She told me that Jess was pregnant and probably wouldn't come back from leave. Then something really weird and unexpected happened. Cindy started telling me a lot of personal information about Jess. It was wildly uncomfortable, and I couldn't see why telling me this was relevant, professional, or even okay to do. That's when I started to think that something felt wrong with this situation. Maybe it was my relationship with Cindy or her relationship with Jess, but either way, I shouldn't be hearing anything about Jess's personal life from Cindy, and she certainly shouldn't gleefully tell me that Jess may be leaving the company.

When Cindy left the next day, I went to Jess and had a very frank conversation with her. I said that Cindy let me know that she hated my team and me, and I would like to know what I did to cause that.

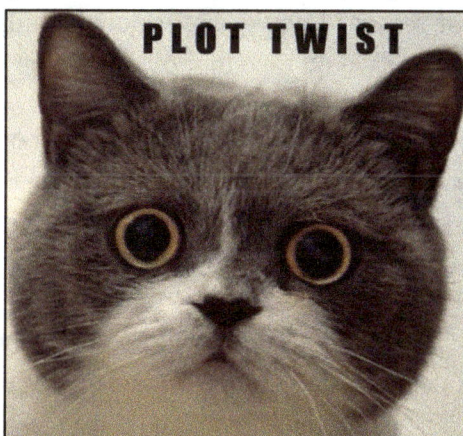

PLOT TWIST

To this day, 20 years later, I remember the look on Jess's face when I walked into her office and asked her why she hated me.

After getting over the shock, she looked at me straight in the eyes and said, "I could ask you the same thing."

Yep.

We got played.

For some reason, Cindy decided that it would be fun to tell Jess bad things about me and tell me bad things about Jess. I have no idea what her end game was, but I am still kicking myself for not talking to Jess long before that final uncomfortable conversation with Cindy.

The rest of the conversation was actually pretty good. We discovered that 99% of what Cindy said was pure *bullshit*. She literally made things up about both of us and if you recall from the list of what a good leader looks like, being a lying *asshole* wasn't on that list. So yes, Jess is the leader that I had that shaped my expectations of leadership.

What was so great about Jess? Well, first of all, she didn't confront me about Cindy because she was trying to be respectful. The version of me that she was getting was pretty dismal. Poor single mom, struggling to stay afloat and resentful that I didn't get the job when my boss was fired. OK, so the poor single mom struggling to stay afloat part was true, but the resentful part, not at all. I honestly had no idea what that role even entailed. One of the reasons I was excited about having a new leader was to learn more about what it would take to move up in the world.

Second, once we got things figured out and cleared the air, Jess didn't hold anything against me. She said that we could start with a clean slate, and she meant it. We had an honest-to-goodness reset. We started meeting regularly, and she got to know my team and me. Finally!

Jess is really smart and innovative. She walked into the office each day with a positive attitude and a mindset of process improvement. It was something that I hadn't ever seen, and it was fascinating. Jess never met a problem that she couldn't solve because of that mindset, and it was something that, as a leader, she passed down to her team.

When I went to Jess with a question about what I should do, she asked me what I thought I should do. The first time it happened, I was taken aback because I was used to someone telling me what to do if I asked for help. Sensing that, she told me that if I wanted to move forward in my career, I had to start finding my own solutions. That was incredibly empowering. After a while, I finally got to a place where I would bring the question along with my possible solution and rather than telling me if the solution was sound or not, Jess would talk me through the pros and cons of my solution. I didn't realize it at the time, but she was actually coaching me towards having the ability to critically think and problem-solve effectively.

Another thing that was incredibly important to my career success was Jess's response to my whining and complaining, which I did a lot of. I was young, and to me, everything was done stupidly, and it annoyed me tremendously. I would complain to Jess, and she would ask me what I planned to do about it. And as you can imagine, I had no plan. I was just pointing out flaws in different processes and situations. I never thought past the complaint to the solution because I had never been empowered to make any changes.

She put an end to that quickly. She told me that if I brought a complaint, I had to bring 3 possible solutions. This started off small, with me bringing little things and fairly weak solutions. Jess would ask me questions about how I arrived at the solution—what was my thought process, who did I talk to so that I could be sure that my solution worked for everyone involved, not just me. This was taking my critical thinking skills to new heights.

The way that she helped me grow and develop was entirely different from what I was used to. In fact, the way that she behaved as a leader was nothing like I'd seen before. It was off-putting at first. I was annoyed that she wasn't just answering my questions, and I felt like she was making me do the legwork that she should be doing as my boss. Thankfully, Jess had a lot of patience and gave me the why behind what she was doing. It went from being disconcerting to eye-opening. I had a leader who deliberately made sure that I could stand on my own two feet. She cared both about my career progression and the progression of my mind, which was all new to me.

The other thing that stands out is that Jess asked me what I wanted to learn from her, and she told me what she wanted to learn from me. That was shocking because I never had a manager say that I had anything they wanted to learn from me. Even if she was faking it and she thought me to be a complete idiot, it didn't show. She seemed to have a genuine curiosity about parts of the job that she wasn't yet a subject matter expert in. Our one-on-one meetings turned into conversations about improvement. Improving the department, the company, and our knowledge base.

As I said earlier, I was absolutely a struggling single mom. Most managers that I'd had before didn't really care about making any sort of accommodations when my son was sick, or daycare was closed or the myriad of other inconvenient things that happen and take you away from work when you have children. They wanted a butt in a chair from 8-5 Monday-Friday.

Jess had a different perspective. She put more of an emphasis on getting the work well than when the work was done. She was the first person who gave me a different view of what working hard meant. To her, it meant being productive and efficient, not how long you were at the office. She suggested taking something home to finish it, which was almost unheard of at that time. Trusting someone to get something done when you weren't able to look over their shoulder wasn't something that I saw every day. People staying late, stretching out their work to make it seem like they were busy and leaving 3 minutes after the manager left was something that I saw every day.

I remember when we had a big project, and for a few months, the whole team had to come in every other Sunday to get things done for a Monday afternoon deadline. I was extremely anxious about it because getting consistent childcare on weekends was hard and expensive. I was pretty nervous to talk to Jess about the dilemma because I didn't want to come off like I was making an excuse. I didn't want to pay the mommy tax and have my career stifled because of something like this. Thankfully, I was able to have a great conversation, and we found a workable solution together. She suggested bringing him with me. And it worked.

The small things mattered. Jess knew I didn't want a free day off. I wanted a gift certificate for groceries, toys, cash. She knew what was important to me personally and professionally. She understood that recognizing me publicly was a major no-no. She was aware that if I was given a 5k bonus, I'd ask to have it split with the rest of the team. She knew that after a while, I would teach someone else everything she had taught me.

Was Jess perfect? No, of course not. But she created a safe space, asked for feedback, and demonstrated that she worked towards strengthening her leadership skills based on the feedback that she was given. She admitted when she was wrong, when she didn't know something, and when, on that rare occasion, she'd actually made a mistake. She was a great leader and had I known how few of them I'd have in my career, I would have tried to soak up much more from her than I did.

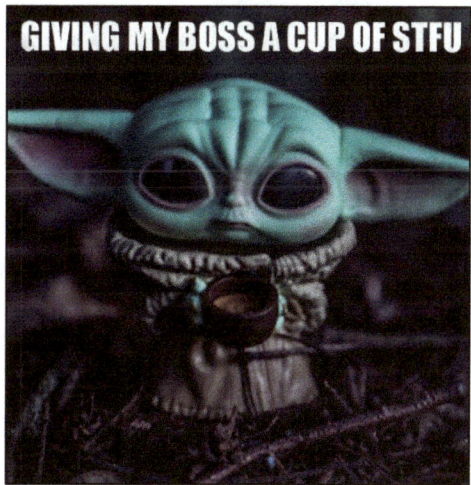

In the 20 years since then, I've had middle managers, and *asshole bosses*. The good thing is that because I had such a great leader early on, I was still able to learn from the bad ones, even if it was just a long list of things to never do. I've grown as a leader, and

I've been able to help other leaders grow and develop. And I owe it all to Jess.

The choice is entirely yours. You know what it takes to be a *kick ass* leader, and you know that it is a lot of work and doesn't happen overnight. If you're currently an *asshole boss*, you're starting at a deficit, so even getting to zero will seem like a major accomplishment. But don't stop there. Push yourself, especially if no one else is pushing you.

The goodness that you can bring into the world is limitless. Each person that you inspire and motivate can turn around and do the same thing for 3 other people, and so on, and so on. *Kick ass* leaders create a ripple effect of positive change in the workplace, spilling into people creating positive changes outside of the workplace at home. Your leadership is critical in making the world a better place.

The world needs *kick ass* leaders because there's already an abundance of *asshole bosses*.

# ASK ME ANYTHING

On Tuesdays, I post *Ask Me Anything* on LinkedIn. There, I answer questions about leadership development, HR, and things of that nature. Over the years, I have received some very interesting questions which I would like to share here along with how I answered them.

## Questions & Answers

### 1. QUESTION FROM ANONYMOUS.

*This individual chose to remain anonymous once he found out the name of the book, which I totally get. Not everyone is comfortable with calling managers assholes.*

**Do you believe leadership qualities are similar over a variety of roles? If not, how can one learn and still instill the traits to adapt and be a good leader in that instant?**

ANSWER: I do think that leadership qualities are similar over a variety of roles. I feel like it's a misconception to think that leadership of, say engineering, is different from leadership in finance. One of the reasons I feel this way is because I see leadership as a personalized experience regardless of what industry you're in.

EXPANDED ANSWER: To add to the original answer, I think that all leadership roles have similar qualities. Whether technical leads, retail leaders, or hospitality leaders, it's all about having the ability to help coach, mentor, and develop people. Someone may not have the technical skills to help an engineer do their job, but the actual leadership qualities to help someone with their personal and professional growth are pretty universal.

## 2. QUESTION FROM ANEESH SURIA

Aneesh is a vehicle powertrain engineer.
*https://www.linkedin.com/in/aneesh-suri/*

***Do you think leadership qualities are dependent on a person's life experiences?***

ANSWER: Ah, really good question!! I think that for some people, they have a high degree of empathy and trust. They can listen to other people's life experiences and learn from them, which helps them grow as a leader. For some other people, they may need to face things head-on to learn from them, those are the people who may struggle a bit more with growth and developing good leadership qualities.

EXPANDED ANSWER: The longer answer to this question is that many personality traits and quirks stem directly from people's life experiences. These quirks, good and bad, can include their leadership qualities. Sometimes when one's life experiences include overcoming obstacles and adversity; it can shape their leadership qualifies in a good or bad way. Sometimes overcoming problems can contribute to people's bias and prejudice, and sometimes it does the exact opposite and helps someone become more aware of some of their shortcomings. I found this question to be very interesting because it hits on something that's a huge part of leadership, accepting and empathizing with the lived experiences of others— even if they are completely unfathomable to you.

## 3. QUESTION FROM KATHERINE SPINNEY

Katherine is a coach and colleague who also does a lot of leadership development.
*https://www.linkedin.com/in/coach-katherine-spinney/*

***I often read that, when hiring, we make our decision almost immediately, yet we proceed with the lengthy hiring process. How much time is really needed before choosing?***

ANSWER: Interesting question. For me, personally, I never make a hiring decision quickly. I feel like when someone does that, they think they are going on instinct.     But really, they are going on bias. Hiring decisions shouldn't be snap decisions. Each candidate should be given equal opportunity and decisions made based on the value that the person brings and their ability to execute in the role.

FOLLOW-UP QUESTION: Tamica Sears, yes! Bias plays such a huge part. Also, confirmation bias. I've read that we make an initial impression and then interpret the rest of the interview based on that initial impression. For example, we like a candidate, so we dismiss some yellow flags along the way, but if we don't initially like them, we turn them to red. Since so much of it is psychology and human nature, I wonder how we can overcome this.

ANSWER: Being aware of it helps. I'm all for taking tons of notes and having many people interview and calibrate. That also helps us answer whether this is a bias or a fact. Like with most things, being open to being wrong is important.

EXPANDED ANSWER: What makes this question even more interesting is that many companies complain about the lack of qualified candidates—yet the process many candidates have to go through is ridiculously long and cumbersome. I'm vehemently opposed to pre-employment testing. A good interview should be able to tell if you the person can do the job. Prolonged testing, especially having them do a case study or presentation, is essentially asking them to work for you for free, which isn't okay. I had to do that once, and it was nerve-wracking, to say the least. I'm pretty sure I gave them the playbook for completing the project they were working on. It was a big factor in my decision to not accept the job offer.

## 4. QUESTION FROM MELISSA FUNDERBURK

Melissa is a DEI Consultant.
*https://www.linkedin.com/in/melissaaaf/*

### *How come you chose HR?*

ANSWER: I didn't choose the thug life; the thug life chose me. Seriously. My first job in high school was as a personnel clerk, doing payroll and filing. The rest is history!

EXPANDED ANSWER: I expanded on this a bit more in other posts, but the main point is that I stumbled into a career that I love because my sister gave me an after-school job working with her. It shaped my life in ways that I couldn't have possibly imagined at the time. It helped me see that there were options available to me that I had never been exposed to otherwise. I know that for some people, hearing representation matters doesn't mean much, but it meant a lot to me. Growing up, it was hard for me to picture myself in jobs that I didn't see other people who looked like me doing. Without it being said, it felt like the jobs that I saw other Black women doing were available to me, and the ones that I didn't were not. It's easy to look back today and say that I was being silly or that the way that I felt didn't make any sense. But tell that to a 12-year-old girl who thinks that her future is limited to what she knows to be true based on her life experiences? I was lucky that I had a sister who could get me an after-school job, and I hit the jackpot when it turned out to be something that I really liked doing and turned into a lifelong career.

## 5. QUESTION FROM ALDO CAVERO

Aldo is a leader at a boutique staffing agency.
*https://www.linkedin.com/in/aldo-cavero-7a3a5796/*

***What do you see as the most effective way of an agency engaging and reaching out to HR leaders (prior to any relationship being formed)? Have there been any memorable examples?***

ANSWER: Send food. Okay, serious answer. An agency once sent me five free resumes of people to reach out to because they saw that I reposted the same position several times. That's the person I want to give my money to. Someone who starts out by looking out for me. A good example of this was when Kenyan Hicks, founder of Broadwing Technical recruiting Company, took a leap of faith and sent me over a few resumes of very qualified people, one of which we made an offer to. He continues to be a shining example for me of how companies should be run.

https://www.linkedin.com/in/kenyan-hicks-48263774/

## 6. QUESTION FROM RIKESHIA DAVISON

Rikeshia is one of the most talented people on LinkedIn when it comes to HBCU recruitment.

https://www.linkedin.com/in/rikeshiaatinternshipseason/

*Happy Tuesday, Tamica! Plenty of companies have had dumpster fire situations over the usual issues: race & pay, racism, sexism, misaligned messaging. If you were HR Manager at one of those companies, how would you support employees during any of those situations? Or, is there a very specific action you WOULD NOT take?*

ANSWER: HR Managers have it rough because they need to take care of the employees and the leaders. Helping leaders to recognize and correct any bias that they have can be rough. I'd be launching 360s like crazy. Also:

- I would try to make sure that if we say bring your whole self to work, we mean it. We can't ask someone to be themselves and then punish them when they are, which happens a lot.

- I would get each and every Caucasian employee accustomed to being called out if their behavior is biased or racist. You don't get to be mad at someone for letting you know that they were mistreated by you.

- I would have clear and consistent messaging about what behavior won't be tolerated, and if there is a violation, even if it is your best performer, they would have the same consequences as anyone else.

- I would NOT assume anyone's race to give them targeted messaging. People of color are a wide range of "colors," and assuming can lead to disaster.

- I would NOT try to implement policies that imply talking about "political" things such as race.

In addition to what was stated above, I'd like to add that I think that HR needs to lead the way when it comes to working through any of the ism's and help each company understand the definition of each by comprehending the difference between some of these things and prejudice and bias. Only then can they help the company break down some of the existing barriers because of deep-seated issues in company policies and procedures.

# ABOUT THE AUTHOR

Tamica Sears, *The Corporate Fixer*, is a Human Resources professional with over 20 years of experience working with Fortune 500 companies in multiple industries. She helps leaders navigate the shifting landscape of corporate America and learn to motivate and inspire the people around them to transform their organizations into more inclusive and innovative places to work. She has guided organizations through mergers and acquisitions, organizational restructures, strategy sessions, succession planning, and creating and implementing leadership development programs. She is a certified Executive and Leadership Development Coach with a PCC accreditation from the ICF and a record of success in serving clients.

Identifying self-esteem as a common issue with many leaders, Tamica published *You Are Enough*, a book of motivational quotes designed to increase self-esteem in 30 days. She has been a guest on numerous podcasts, led workshops, and spoken at conferences about leadership development; diversity, equity, and inclusion; the future of work; personal branding; and self-awareness.

Tamica provides HR Consulting and Executive Coaching for small businesses, helping leaders become better equipped to transform organizational cultures to be more innovative and inclusive while enabling their teams to be more responsive to changes in the environment and be more engaged and productive. She loves working with HR teams to help them become value-added business partners, rather than administrative compliance cops.